Contents

General Principles
of EC Law

■ EUROPEAN LAW SERIES ■

Series Editor:
PROFESSOR JOHN A. USHER

General Principles
of EC Law

Addison Wesley Longman Limited
Edinburgh Gate
Harlow, Essex CM20 2JE
England
and Association Companies throughout the world

*Published in the United States of America
by Addison Wesley Longman Inc., New York*

First published 1998

ISBN 0 582 27749-3 Paper

British Library Cataloguing-in-Publication Data
A catalogue record for this book is
available from the British Library

Library of Congress Cataloging-in-Publication Data
A catalog entry for this title is available from the
Library of Congress

Set by 7 in 10/12pt Sabon

Produced by Longman Singapore Publishers Pte Ltd

Printed in Singapore

Foreword

Without wishing to anticipate the discussion on the nature of General Principles of Community Law in Chapter 1 of this book, it may be suggested that the development of these general principles is one of the clearest illustrations of the fact that Community Law does not exist in a legal vacuum. The very real interaction between Community law and the national laws of the Member States, though not the only source of general principles of Community law, has long been a matter of fascination to me. My first article on Community law as such (published, I regret to have to confess, more than twenty years ago) was on the influence of national concepts on decisions of the European Court of Justice, and my inaugural lecture when I was appointed to the Chair of European Law in the University of Exeter (more than ten years ago) was on the converse subject of the indirect influence of principles of Community law within the legal systems of the UK. In many ways this book can be regarded as having developed out of those ideas – and to the extent that they remain relevant, I have unashamedly repeated them.

One thing which will become apparent from this book is that not all general principles of Community law, particularly those concerned with good administration, can be regarded as concerned with fundamental rights, and it is not my intention to deal with fundamental rights as such. In the context of the present series, therefore, this book should be read in conjunction with the volume by Lammy Betten and Nicholas Grief on *EU Law and Human Rights*.

This book could not have been produced without the support of my wife, who must have thought that she had lost me into the embrace of a computer while it and its companion volume on *EC*

Institutions and Legislation were completed. It also would not have produced without the steady and patient persuasion of Brian Willan at Addison Wesley Longman.

The law is stated as at the beginning of January 1998, and account has been taken of the text of the Treaty of Amsterdam signed on 2 October 1997.

John A. Usher
Europa Institute
University of Edinburgh
January 1998.

General Editor's Preface

The Longman European Law Series is the first comprehensive series of topic-based books on EC Law aimed primarily at a student readership, though I have no doubt that they will also be found useful by academic colleagues and interested practitioners. It has become more and more difficult for a single course or a single book to deal comprehensively with all the major topics of Community law, and the intention of this series is to enable students and teachers to 'mix and match' topics which they find to be of interest; it may also be hoped that the publication of this series will encourage the study of areas of Community law which have historically been neglected in degree courses. However, while the series may have a student readership in mind, the authors have been encouraged to take an academic and critical approach, placing each topic in its overall Community context, and also in its socio-economic and political context where relevant.

The general principles of EC law discussed in this book underlie all areas of Community activity, and show very clearly the extent to which there is mutual influence between Community law and the national legal systems of the Member States – and indeed the creative role played by the European Court of Justice in the developemnt of Community law.

John A. Usher

Table of Cases

xi

Table of Treaty Provisions

CHAPTER ONE

The development of general principles

Introduction

One can ... summarise the situation by saying that the general principles of Community law have evolved under the pressure of having to reach decisions in relation to matters not expressly covered by the Treaties and that those principles are extrapolated from the Treaties and from the currents of thought in the legal systems of Member States as at the time of the decision.[1]

Treaty recognition of this judge-made law came in the incorporation into the Maastricht Treaty on European Union of an express obligation to respect the principles underlying the European Convention on Human Rights and the fundamental rights flowing from national constitutions as 'general principles of Community law'. This has been taken further in the 1997 Amsterdam Treaty, which expressly mentions what is perhaps the best known of these general principles, the principle of proportionality, in its Protocol on Subsidiarity

It should, however, be said at the outset that this book is not concerned with fundamental rights as such, although particularly clear examples of the development of general principles of Community law may be found in that area; nor is this book concerned with the development of case-law concepts such as direct effect or the primacy of Community law, which go to the heart of the institutional structure of the EC. Rather, it is concerned with the way in which the European Court has developed general principles

---

[1.] Lord Justice Schiemann, 'The Application of General Principles of Community Law by English Courts', The European Advocate, Winter Issue 1996/7, pp. 4–10.

I

of law derived from the national legal systems of the Member States, from the EC Treaty itself, or from international agreements to which Member States are parties, as a method of interpreting or determining the validity of acts of Community institutions, as a control mechanism over the actions of Community institutions, as a control mechanism over the acts of national authorities when they are acting within the scope of Community law, and quite simply to fill the gaps in the Community legal order.

Recognition of general principles

Maastricht (TEU)

While Article F of the Treaty on European Union requires the Union to respect the principles underlying the European Convention on Human Rights and the fundamental rights flowing from national constitutions as 'general principles of *Community* law', the only express reference in the European Community Treaty itself to Community law being derived from principles of national law may be found in Article 215(2). This provides that the Community institutions may incur non-contractual liability 'in accordance with the general principles common to the laws of the Member States', and its use will be considered later in this book. It may, however, be observed that in the context of the contractual liability of the Community institutions, the European Court may actually find itself applying rules of national law as such, rather than deriving principles of Community law from them, since contractual liability depends on the law governing the contract, and the European Court only has jurisdiction if that is conferred by the terms of the contract. By way of example, the Court has found itself having to construe the Belgian law of construction contracts in relation to a building erected in Italy for Euratom.[2]

More generally, the Treaties have from the start required that 'the Court shall ensure that in the interpretation and application of this Treaty, and of the rules laid down for the implementation thereof, the law is observed'. This formula was first used in Article 31 of the Treaty establishing the European Coal and Steel Community, and is repeated (with the omission of the phrase 'and of the rules laid down for the implementation thereof', which in itself has been of no practical significance) in Article 164 of the Treaty

---

[2.] Case 318/81 *Commission v Co. DE. MI* [1985] ECR 3663.

establishing the European Community and in Article 136 of the Treaty establishing the European Atomic Energy Community.

Early in the history of the Court of Justice of the Coal and Steel Community, as it then was, it was realised that the express Treaty provisions and the rules laid down for their implementation were not necessarily sufficiently comprehensive to resolve disputes which might arise within the context of the Community. As A.G. Lagrange pointed out in his opinion in Case 8/55 *Fédération Charbonnière de Belgique v High Authority*,[3] citing Article 4 of the French Civil Code,[4] the Court could not be absolved from giving judgment because of a lacuna in Community law. Even before this, it had been stated by A.G. Roemer in his Opinion in Case 6/54 *Netherlands v High Authority*[5] that account must be taken of the law of the different Member States in order to interpret Community law.

Indeed, in one of the leading staff cases[6] to arise under the ECSC Treaty, the Court went so far as to mention specifically rules applicable in the law of individual Member States to the situation before it. In the case, *inter alia*, the Court had to decide whether certain decisions of the Assembly (now the European Parliament) as to staff grading could be revoked, which, as it said, was a problem of administrative law well known in all the then Member States, but which was not provided for by the Treaty. The Court added that unless it was to commit a denial of justice, the problem would have to be resolved on the basis of rules recognised by legislation, academic authorities and case-law in the Member States. The Court found that if the act in question were legal, and individual rights had been acquired under it, then it could not be revoked, because of the need to protect the expectations thus created (a concept of which more will be said). On the other hand, it was found that if the act was illegal, then all the Member States recognised that it could be revoked, with variations notably as to the time during which this could be done, and the Court made specific reference to the provisions of French, German and Italian law in this respect. This is still cited as authority, although it has now

---

3. [1954 to 1956] ECR 245 at pp. 277–8.
4. 'le juge qui refusera de juger, sous prétexte du silence, de l'obscurité ou de l'insuffisance de la loi, pourra être poursuivi comme coupable de déni de justice.'
5. [1954 to 1956] ECR 103 at p. 118.
6. Joined Cases 7/56 and 3-7/57 *Algera and others v Assembly* [1957 and 1958] ECR 39 at pp. 55–6.

become linked with the better-known and broader principle of the protection of legitimate expectations, as in Case C-90/95P *De Compte v European Parliament.*[7]

Whilst a similar exercise was carried out with regard to the scope of property rights in Case 44/79 *Hauer v Land Rheinland–Pfalz,*[8] it is perhaps more common to find specific provisions of national legal systems discussed in the Opinions of Advocates General rather than in the Court's judgments.

One of the main reasons why the European Court became used to hearing arguments based on concepts of national law was (and is) Article 177 of the EC Treaty, enabling courts in Member States to refer questions of interpretation of Community acts to the Court of Justice for a preliminary ruling. In the first reference heard under this Article, Case 13/61 *De Geus v Bosch,*[9] an appeal had been lodged against the decision of the domestic court, and the question arose as to the effect of the appeal on the reference (a question, incidentally, that has had to be considered on several subsequent occasions). The point is not covered by Article 177, but rather than consider the matter in the abstract, A. G. Lagrange discussed the practice in those Member States whose domestic systems use a preliminary ruling procedure, notably France and Germany, to conclude that the mere lodging of an appeal did not affect the existence of the reference;[10] the Court, for its part, succinctly noted that its jurisdiction was dependent solely on the existence of a request for a preliminary ruling,[11] a view it has continued to take in this area.

For the most part, however, the national concepts used by the Court are themselves more general in nature – what in the original Member States was termed 'unwritten law' – although in Case 108/63 *Merlini v High Authority,*[12] where the applicant claimed that the High Authority was estopped from fixing the equalisation contributions due from the applicants on the ground that it had earlier asked for a smaller sum, the Court found it necessary to state specifically that 'the fact that such a rule' (i.e. estoppel) 'is not mentioned in written law is not sufficient proof that it does not exist'.

[7.] 17 April 1997.
[8.] [1979] ECR 3727.
[9.] [1962] ECR 45.
[10.] Ibid at pp. 58–61.
[11.] Ibid at p. 50.
[12.] [1965] ECR 1 at p. 10.

Furthermore, it is worth noting that since 1974 the Court has felt itself able at least in the matter of fundamental rights even to take account of rules derived from *international* law in so far as they are binding upon the Member States – in effect therefore as principles common to the laws of the Member States. In Case 4/73 *Nold v Commission*,[13] where the applicant alleged the infringement of its property rights and its right to the free pursuit of business activity, the Court stated that fundamental rights form an integral part of the general principles of law of which it ensures the observance and in safeguarding which it is bound to draw inspiration from constitutional traditions common to the Member States, and added: 'international treaties for the protection of human rights on which the Member States have collaborated or of which they are signatories, can supply guidelines which should be followed within the framework of Community law.'

More specifically, in Case 36/75 *Rutili v Ministre de l'Intérieur*,[14] a reference for a preliminary ruling made in an action brought by an Italian national against the French authorities challenging restrictions placed on his right of residence in France as a result, *inter alia*, of his participation in certain trade union activities, the Court, after referring to the restrictions imposed by the Community legislation on the powers of Member States to control migrant workers, stated that: 'these limitations ... are a specific manifestation of the more general principle, enshrined in Articles 8, 9, 10 and 11 of the Convention for the Protection of Human Rights and Fundamental Freedoms, signed in Rome on 4 November 1950 and ratified by all the Member States, and in Article 2 of Protocol No. 4 of the same Convention.' Even in the context of private law, it may be observed that particular reference has been made to the Human Rights Convention with reference to the delimitation of property rights.[15]

With regard to the use which may be made of these general principles, it is apparent from *Rutili* that, as a matter of public law, these fundamental rights and general principles may be invoked not simply against Community institutions but also against national authorities to the extent that they are acting in a Com-

---

13. [1974] ECR 491 at p. 507.
14. [1975] ECR 1219.
15. See Case 44/79 *Hauer v Land Rheinland–Pfalz* [1979] ECR 3727.

munity law context.[16] On the other hand, the Court has no jurisdiction to consider the compatibility of national legislation with
the Human Rights Convention where it falls within an area which
is still a matter of national competence. Hence, in Case 60/84
Cinéthèque v Fédération Nationale des Cinémas Français,[17] the
European Court held that it had no power to consider whether
French legislation, prohibiting the marketing of video-cassettes
within a fixed period of a film being released for cinema showing,
constituted a breach of the principle of freedom of expression set
out in Article 10 of the European Human Rights Convention.
While that statement is in itself unexceptionable, it does raise the
awkward question of determining when a Member State is acting
entirely under national competence: in *Cinéthèque* itself there is
scope for debate as to whether the French legislation fell outside
the scope of the free movement of goods rules or constituted a
'mandatory requirement' under the *Cassis de Dijon* case-law.[18] Be
that as it may, it is clear that when a Member State is acting under
an express Treaty derogation it is acting within the scope of Community law and therefore bound by the principles derived from the
Human Rights Convention, as was reaffirmed in the Greek Broadcasting case in 1991.[19] It was there held that where a Member
State was invoking the public policy exception under Articles 56
and 66 in relation to a supply of services (i.e. broadcasts) from
other Member States, its legislation must respect the principle of
freedom of expression laid down in Article 10 of the Convention
as a general principle of Community law. On the other hand, the
situation of someone who has not exercised Community law rights
and has only a purely hypothetical prospect of so doing does not
fall within the field of application of Community law, and, as was
held in Case C-299/95 *Kremzow v Austria*,[20] the European Court
cannot therefore respond to a reference for a preliminary ruling as
to the conformity of national legislation with the fundamental
rights whose observance the Court ensures.

While the general principles of Community law derived from in-

---

16. See also Case 222/84 *Johnstone v Chief Constable of the Royal Ulster
Constabulary* [1986] ECR 1651 in relation to national measures under the
Equal Treatment Directive (Council Directive 76/207).
17. [1985] ECR 2605.
18. See Green, Hartley and Usher, *The Legal Foundations of the Single European
Market* (Oxford, 1991) pp. 70–1.
19. Case C-260/89 *Elliniki Radiophonia Tiléorassi* [1991] ECR I–2925.
20. 29 May 1997.

ternational law have largely involved Treaty provisions, in particular the European Convention on Human Rights, nevertheless the general principle of good faith in public international law has been held by the Court of First Instance to give rise to legitimate expectations in Community law. In Case T-115/94 *Opel Austria v Council*,[21] it was held that once the Community had deposited its instruments of approval of the European Economic Area Agreement and the date of its entry into force was known, a trader was entitled, as a corollary to the principle of good faith in public international law, to form the legitimate expectation that the Community would not introduce measures affecting it in the intervening period contrary to the terms of the European Economic Area Agreement.

General principles in common use

Identification

Some concepts derived from national sources have now become so well established in the case-law of the Court that they have become principles of Community law in their own right. Indeed, the principle of proportionality has been expressly elevated to Treaty status by the Treaty of Amsterdam 1997, introducing a Protocol on the application of the principles of subsidiarity and proportionality. Article 1 of this Protocol requires each institution to 'ensure compliance with the principle of proportionality, according to which any action by the Community shall not go beyond what is necessary to achieve the objectives of the Treaty'. More generally, in Case 112/77 *Töpfer*[22] it was said that the principle of legitimate expectation formed part of the Community legal order, and hence that failure to respect a legitimate expectation would be a breach of the Treaty within the meaning of Article 173. However, principles derived from national law may still be distinguished from those general principles of Community law derived from the Treaties as such, examples of the latter being, in external trade, the concept of Community preference,[23] in social affairs, the notion of equality of treatment of nationals of other Member States, which has been generalised from the provisions of

21. [1997] ECR II-39.
22. [1978] ECR 1019.
23. See Case 5/67 *Beus v Hauptzollamt München* [1968] ECR 83 at p. 98 invoking EC Treaty, Article 44(2).

the EC Treaty relating to the free movement of workers [24] and the right of establishment,[25] in business law the requirement that competition should not be eliminated,[26] and, between Member States, the duty of 'solidarity'.[27]

One problem which is encountered in listing those principles of Community law which have been derived from national sources is that in some cases what is in effect the same principle may be known by more than one name, but a few examples may be given. They include the concept of good faith,[28] the right to be heard, developed in the context of the *Transocean*[29] case, and reaffirmed in the context of anti-dumping procedure in the *Al-Jubail Fertilizer* case,[30] and 'force majeure', the precise meaning of which, according to the Court, has to be decided by reference to the legal context in which it is intended to operate, but which is not limited to absolute impossibility;[31] indeed, in one case[32] the Court implied a 'force majeure' clause into a Regulation that did not contain one, on the basis that such clauses were contained in parallel Regulations. The Court has also considered a doctrine of estoppel, sometimes under the Latin tag *'non venire contra factum proprium'*, though it has rarely applied it.[33] It has, however, applied a concept of unjust enrichment,[34] has given a Community definition of legitimate self-protection (the 'légitime défense' of French-derived systems),[35] has, in staff disciplinary matters,[36] and more generally,[37]

---

24. See Case 152/73 *Sotgiu v Deutsche Bundespost* [1974] ECR 153 at p. 164.
25. See Case 2/74 *Reyners v. Belgium* [1974] ECR 631 at p. 651.
26. Derived from Articles 2, 3, 85 and 86 of the EEC Treaty: see Case 6/72 *Europemballage and Continental Can v Commission* [1973] ECR 215 at p. 244; Joined Cases 6 and 7/63 *Commercial Solvents v Commission* [1974] ECR 223 at p. 252.
27. See Case 39/72 *Commission v Italy* [1973] ECR 101 at p. 116; [1973] CMLR 439.
28. See e.g. Case 44/59 *Fiddelaar v Commission* [1960] ECR 535 at p. 547.
29. Case 17/74 *Transocean Marine Paint Association v Commission* [1974] ECR 1063.
30. Case C-49/88, [1991] ECR I-3187.
31. Case 158/73 *Kampffmeyer v Einfuhr und Vorratsstelle für Getreide* [1974] ECR 101 at p. 110.
32. Case 64/74 *Reich v Hauptzollamt Landau* [1975] ECR 261 at pp. 268–9; [1975] 1 CMLR 396.
33. See e.g. Joined Cases 17 and 20/61 *Klöckner v High Authority* [1962] ECR 325 at p. 342. For an application, see Case 6/72 *Europemballage v Commission* [1973] ECR 215 at p. 241; [1973] CMLR 199.
34. Case 36/72 *Meganck v Commission* [1962] ECR 289 at p. 303.
35. Case 16/61 *Modena v High Authority* [1962] ECR 289 at p. 303.
36. Joined Cases 18 and 35/65 *Gutmann v Commission* [1966] ECR 103 at p. 119.
37. Case C-137/85 *Maizena II* [1987] ECR 4587 at para. 23.

applied the rule (*non bis in idem*) that a person may not be punished twice for the same offence, and has accepted the principle of *nulla poena sine lege*, under which penalties cannot be imposed unless they are founded on a clear and unambiguous legal basis.[38]

In early decisions under the ECSC Treaty, reference was made in several cases to the French concept of 'égalité devant les charges publiques',[39] but this now seems largely to be subsumed in the wider principle of equality of treatment or non-discrimination,[40] which is regarded as a general principle flowing from the Treaties. This principle was held to be breached by a regulation which, after a production refund had been paid for many years both on maize used for starch and on maize groats and meal, retained it only for the former.[41]

Express reference to general principles

As mentioned above, the only express mention of general principles derived from the laws of the Member States is in Article 215 of the EC Treaty (and Article 188 of the Euratom Treaty), which provides that in the case of non-contractual liability, the Community shall, 'in accordance with the general principles common to the laws of the Member State, make good any damage caused by its institutions or by its servants in the performance of their duties'. The consequences of this phrase may be illustrated in relation to liability for harm caused by legislation.

It was established in 1971 that in order to recover damages for harm caused by a legislative act of a Community institution, it was necessary to show that a 'sufficiently serious violation of a superior rule of law for the protection of the individual has occurred'.[42] In his Opinion in that case, A. G. Roemer made reference to a conference on the liability of the State for the wrongful conduct of its institutions held at the Max-Planck Institute in 1964,[43] and suggested that the requirement to have regard to the general principles common to the laws of the Member States should not be taken too

---

38. Case C-14/81, *Alphasteel* [1982] ECR 768 at para. 29.
39. See Joined Cases 14, 16, 17, 20, 24, 26 and 27/60 and 1/61 *Meroni v High Authority* [1961] ECR 161 at p. 169.
40. See e.g. Case 148/73 *Louwage v Commission* [1974] ECR 81 at p. 89.
41. Cases 124/76 and 20/77 *Moulins de Pont-à-Mousson* [1977] ECR 1795.
42. Originally formulated in Case 5/71 *Zuckerfabrik Schöppenstedt v Council* [1971] ECR 975 at p. 984.
43. See [1971] ECR at p. 989.

literally; rather, what was indicated was a process of assessment taking account of the particular objectives of the Treaty and the peculiarities of the Community structure, and he concluded that the guideline should be the 'best-elaborated national rules'.

However, in 1973, following the Accession of the United Kingdom, Denmark and Ireland, it was argued very strongly on behalf of the Community institutions in Cases 63 to 69/72 *Werhahn and others v Council and Commission*,[44] that, having regard in particular to the legal systems of the new Member States, there was no general legal principle that the Community should be liable for legislative acts. As a matter of substantive law that was possibly true, but what this argument missed was the point made by A. G. Lagrange in an extra-judicial capacity,[45] cited by A. G. Gand in 1969 in Case 9/69 *Sayag v Leduc*,[46] in which he observed that the only truly common legal principle was that which by then disapproved in all Member States of the doctrine of non-liability of the State, i.e. the principle underlying the Crown Proceedings Act. It may be observed that, a quarter of a century later, similar views were expressed by A. G. Léger on the analogous topic of the liability of Member States for breaches of Community law in his Opinion in Case C-5/94 *R v MAFF, ex p Hedley Lomas*.[47] He there observed that 'as far as state liability for legislative action is concerned, there are no general principles which are truly common to the Member States. The principles established by the Court in relation to Article 215 of the Treaty have, in fact, been those laid down by the systems of domestic law most protective of individuals suffering damage through legislative action'. In the light of this approach, the argument may be developed in the context of Article 215(2) that the structure of the Treaties is such as to create Communities whose institutions are answerable for their wrongful acts. Since a large proportion of the acts of the Community institutions are legislative or quasi-legislative in nature, if the institutions were not answerable for their legislative acts, then they would virtually be above the law. To develop a point made by A. G. Roemer in his Opinion in the *Werhahn* case, the idea in the United Kingdom there could be no State liability for legislative acts was very closely correlated to the concept of the sovereignty of Parlia-

---

44. [1973] ECR 1229.
45. 'The non-contractual liability of the Community' (1965–66) CMLRev 32.
46. [1969] ECR at p. 340.
47. [1996] ECR I–2553 at p. 2579.

ment. This was a concept which had very little relevance in the case of legislation which emanated solely from appointed bodies, not from elected ones. Indeed, A. G. Roemer pointed out that this may make it necessary to put special stress on the concept of the strengthening by the Court of legal protection within the Community. Whether the same approach should be applied when certain Community legislation, indeed the majority of internal market legislation, emanates jointly from an elected Parliament and an appointed Council by virtue of the codecision procedure introduced by the Maastricht Treaty and extended by the Treaty of Amsterdam, is a matter which perhaps requires further debate. In the result, in the *Werhahn* case, the Court itself simply repeated the formula it had used in 1971, which would appear to imply that the nature of a 'general principle common to the laws of the Member States' is a matter of Community law determined by the European Court of Justice, whatever the national origins of that principle.

CHAPTER TWO

Principles derived from the Community Treaties

Introduction

Most of the general principles discussed in this book may be regarded as being derived from the national laws of the Member States or as being derived from international law through the medium of the laws of the Member States. There are nevertheless important general principles of Community law which have been derived directly from express provisions of the Community Treaties themselves. At least two different techniques may be observed in this context. One approach is to extrapolate a general principle from a relatively limited Treaty provision; the clearest example of this is the concept of Community preference. On the other hand, where the same concept is expressly stated in a number of different provisions in different parts of the EC Treaty, the European Court may find that such a concept is an underlying general principle of Community law. The prime example of this is the principle of non-discrimination, which is expressly stated, often in considerable detail, in relation to nationality (particularly in the context of the exercise of the basic Treaty freedoms), in relation to internal taxation of goods, in relation to the pay of men and women (and under the Treaty of Amsterdam 1997 also with regard to opportunities and treatment in matters of employment and occupation in general), and in relation to common organisations of agricultural markets. As will be shown later in this chapter, each of those sets of provisions has been held to be an illustration of an underlying general principle of non-discrimination or equality of treatment.

Community preference

The phrase 'Community preference' only appears expressly in the Treaty in Article 44(2), a provision which allowed Member States to introduce a non-discriminatory system of minimum prices during the original transitional period, which expired on 1 January 1970. Article 44(2) refers to 'the development of a natural preference between Member States', and in Case 5/67 *Beus v HZA München*[1] the Court held it to be one of the underlying principles of the Treaty, effectively generalising this very specific illustration of the principle; indeed, it may be suggested that the price structure of most common organisations has inexorably led to Community preference.[2] A particular illustration of the principle may, however, be found in Case 55/75 *Balkan v HZA Berlin-Packhof*,[3] where an importer complained that monetary compensatory amounts, designed to compensate the difference between real rates of exchange and agricultural rates of exchange where there was a risk of disturbances in trade in agricultural products, were imposed on imports of Bulgarian cheese into Germany but not on imports of similar Italian cheese. It was held that, with regard to the cheese coming from Italy, the general principle of Community preference justified a different assessment of the possibilities of disturbance, according to whether the products involved came from another Member State or from a third State. With regard to the treatment of different third States, it was observed in Case 236/84 *Malt v HZA Düsseldorf*,[4] in the context of the imposition of monetary compensatory amounts on beef imported into the Community under a tariff quota, that there was no obligation on the Community to offer the same treatment to different third countries or to products imported from different third countries.

The concept of Community preference may also be linked with the principle of proportionality discussed in Chapter 3. In a dispute involving the validity of a countervailing charge on imports of dried grapes from third countries, it was held[5] that the aim of the

---

1. [1968] ECR 83.
2. See Fennell, 'Community Preference and Developing Countries' (1997) European Foreign Affairs Review 235.
3. [1976] ECR 11.
4. [1986] ECR 1923.
5. Case 77/86 *R v Customs and Excise, ex p National Dried Fruit Trade Association* [1988] ECR 757.

charge was to enforce a minimum price 'so as to ensure Community preference in the market' but not to inflict an economic penalty on a trader who had imported at less than the minimum price; therefore, to impose a fixed-rate charge even where the difference between the import price and the minimum price was very small was disproportionate and amounted to an economic penalty. On the other hand, such a charge is legitimate if it does not exceed the gap between the minimum price and the import price.[6]

It will be evident from this that the principle of Community preference may conflict with other principles of Community law. While it has been doubted whether breach of this principle would invalidate Community legislation,[7] it has nevertheless been regarded as justifying breaches of other trade-related general principles of Community law. An example relates to the creation of the Customs Union in the EC. Just as the EC Treaty made no express provision for the enactment of common rules on the valuation for goods for customs purposes or on the determination of the origin of goods for customs purposes,[8] so also it contained no express prohibition on Member States imposing charges equivalent to customs duties[9] on imports from non-Member States after the Common Customs Tariff entered into force. In practice, the agricultural legislation of the Community does usually expressly prohibit such charges, and such a prohibition is also contained in some of the specific trade arrangements negotiated by the Community, but there is still no general legislative prohibition on such charges. Hence, this is a matter in which the general principles have been laid down in the case-law of the European Court. The matter came before the Court in 1973 in the context of Belgian legislation imposing a charge on imports of rough diamonds from non-Member States for the benefit of the Belgian social fund for diamond workers.[10] Having determined that this was a charge levied only by reason of importation, therefore equivalent in its nature to a customs duty, the Court held that it was clear from the objectives of

---

6. Cases C-351, 352 and 353/93 *Van der Linde* [1995] ECR I-85.
7. Case C-353/92 *Greece v Council* [1994] ECR I-3411. See Chapter * below.
8. See Green, Hartley and Usher, *The Legal Foundations of the Single European Market* (Oxford, 1991) Chapter 1.
9. In effect, a charge other than a customs duty as such levied by reason of crossing a frontier. For a discussion of the concept in the context of internal Community trade see Green, Hartley and Usher, *The Legal Foundations of the Single European Market* (Oxford, 1991) Chapter 3.
10. Cases 37 and 38/73 *Diamantarbeiders v Indiamex* [1973] ECR 1609.

the Common Customs Tariff that Member States could not alter the level of protection defined by that tariff by means of charges supplementing the Common Customs Tariff duties. Furthermore, the Court noted that even if the charge were not protective in nature, nevertheless its very existence could hardly be reconciled with the requirements of a common commercial policy. The Court therefore concluded that Member States could not, following the establishment of the Common Customs Tariff, introduce in a unilateral manner new charges on goods imported directly from third countries or raise the level of those in existence at the time the tariff was introduced. The basic tenor of the Court's judgment appears to be that a Common Customs Tariff and a common commercial policy require uniform external protection at the external frontiers of the Community's Single Market.

However, the possible conflict between this objective and the concept of Community preference came clearly to a head in Case 70/77 *Simmenthal v Italian Finance Administration*,[11] which involved charges levied under Italian legislation in relation to the health inspection of meat imported into Italy from Uruguay. The Court here recognised that it was the Community policy of achieving a uniform external protection which prevented Member States from imposing their own charges having equivalent effect to customs duties on imports from non-Member States, but it accepted that the Council and Commission could create exceptions or derogations for the prohibition on charges having equivalent effect to customs duties provided that the charges involved had a uniform effect in all Member States in trade with third countries. However, in this case the Court was faced with the difficulty that health inspections would have been required in Community internal trade and that under the relevant Community legislation, giving express effect to the concept of Community preference, national provisions relating to imports from third countries were not to be more favourable than those governing intra-Community trade. The Court therefore found itself having to accept that a Member State *must* hold inspections and charge for them where such inspections would be held and could be charged for in internal Community trade. In internal Community trade, such charges are in principle permissible if they do not exceed the actual cost of carrying out the

11. [1978] ECR 1453.

inspection, but the Court in Case 30/79 *Land Berlin v Wigei*[12] had to accept that in order to avoid reverse discrimination against Community products (i.e. to preserve Community preference), the charges imposed for the inspection of products imported from non-Member States could exceed those levied on inspections of Community products provided they were not manifestly disproportionate. Subsequently, the Court has expressly accepted that the lawfulness of imposing a charge for a health inspection could not be subject to the existence of comparable charges in all the other Member States, at least where the charge corresponded to the cost of the inspection;[13] hence, this would appear to amount to an admission that there can be different treatment of imports from non-Member States depending on the Member State into which they are imported.

Applying this principle to other national measures which may be justified in internal Community trade on the grounds specified in Article 36 of the EC Treaty[14] or as 'mandatory requirements' under the *Cassis de Dijon* case-law[15] it is submitted that a Member State not only may, but in fact must, apply such measures in trade with third countries if it applies them in internal Community trade.

Non-discrimination

Nationality

Article 6 of the EC Treaty (formerly Article 7 of the EEC Treaty) prohibits 'any discrimination on the grounds of nationality' within the scope of application of the Treaty, subject to any special provisions set out in the Treaty. This requirement, or a rule requiring equal treatment with home nationals, is expressly repeated in relation to the free movement of workers in Article 48(2), in relation to freedom of establishment in Article 52, and in relation to free-

12. [1980] ECR 151.
13. Case 1/83 *Intercontinentale Fleischhandelsgesellschaft v Bavaria* [1984] ECR 349.
14. See Green, Hartley and Usher, *The Legal Foundations of the Single European Market* (Oxford, 1991) Chapter 7.
15. Case 120/78 *Rewe v Bundesmonopolverwaltung für Branntwein* [1979] ECR 649. See Green, Hartley and Usher, *The Legal Foundations of the Single European Market* (Oxford, 1991) Chapter 6.

dom to provide services in Article 60, at least with regard to those offering a service.

The use of the general principle of non-discrimination on grounds of nationality enounced in Article 6 of the EC Treaty is shown in Case 186/87 *Cowan v Trésor public*.[16] Mr. Cowan, a British citizen, was 'mugged' on a visit to Paris, and made a claim under the French criminal injuries compensation scheme. However, under the French scheme, compensation could only be paid to French nationals, or to nationals of States having reciprocal arrangements with France, or to holders of French residence permits. On a reference to the European Court, it was held that Article [6] requires those who are in a situation governed by Community law to be treated in exactly the same way as nationals of the host State, that, as had already been held in *Luisi and Carbone v Trésor public*,[17] tourists as recipients of services fall within the Treaty freedom to provide services, and that therefore a residence requirement could not be imposed on a tourist from another Member State when it was not imposed on a French national. It was further held that, to the extent that Community law guarantees a person the right to enter another Member State, a corollary of such free movement is that such a person should be protected from harm on the same basis as nationals or residents of that State.

Before the EEC Treaty was transformed into the EC Treaty by the Maastricht amendments, a particularly intriguing use of the principle of non-discrimination in the former Article 7 was in conjunction with the former Article 128 of the EEC Treaty on a common vocational training policy.[18] In Case 152/82 *Forcheri v Belgium*,[19] the Italian wife of a Commission official living in Belgium was charged a special foreign students' fee for following a social work course in Brussels. It was held that, while educational and vocational training policy was not as such a matter of Community competence, the opportunity for, and access to, such courses did fall within the scope of the Treaty, so that Belgium could not require payment of a fee not required of its own nationals.

This was taken further in Case 293/83 *Gravier v City of*

---

16. [1989] ECR 195.
17. Cases 286/82 and 26/83 *Luisi and Carbone* [1984] ECR 377.
18. Now replaced by Article 126 of the EC Treaty on education and Article 127 of the EC Treaty on vocational training.
19. [1983] ECR 2323.

Liège,[20] where it was held that the principle of non-discrimination applied with regard to access to vocational training even in favour of Community nationals who were not previously resident in the State in which the course was offered. The course there at issue involved strip cartoon art, and the Court stated that a course constituted vocational training when the institution prepared its students for a qualification for a particular profession, trade or employment, or provided them with the skills necessary for such profession, trade or employment. This approach was further developed, again with regard to discriminatory tuition fees (the *minerval*), in Case 24/86 *Blaizot*,[21] where the issue was whether university courses in general could be regarded as vocational training. The conclusion reached was that they could, not just where the final academic examination directly provided a professional qualification, but also where a student needed the knowledge so acquired for employment etc., even though there was no legal requirement to have that knowledge. It was held that, in general, University courses meet those criteria, with the exception of courses intended for persons wishing to improve their general knowledge rather than prepare themselves for an occupation. It may therefore be submitted that anyone following a university course with the intention of gaining employment at the end of it was, in Community law, undertaking vocational training.

It has subsequently been affirmed that the different years of a course could not be treated separately in determining whether it constituted vocational training, provided it represented a single whole.[22]

In the most recent of the Belgian *minerval* cases, Case C-47/93 *Commission v Belgium*,[23] the principle of non-discrimination was found to be breached by national provisions giving the rectors of Belgian universities the right to refuse to reimburse non-national EC students for unduly paid *minerval* charges where they did not have the power to refuse repayment to Belgian students: i.e. persons in the same situation were treated differently on the basis of nationality.

While the substance of this case-law may have been overtaken by Article 126 of the EC Treaty on education, the technique of

20. [1985] ECR 593.
21. [1988] ECR 379.
22. Case 263/88 *Humbel* [1988] ECR 5365.
23. [1994] I-ECR 1593.

linking the general principle of non-discrimination in Article 6 with substantive provisions of Community law which are silent on the point remains. Indeed, it has been stated categorically that 'Article [6] of the [EC] Treaty, which lays down as a general principle a prohibition of discrimination on the grounds of nationality, applies independently only to situations governed by Community law in regard to which the Treaty lays down no specific rules prohibiting discrimination'.[24]

A further example of the Court holding a provision of national law to contrary to Article 6 EC is Case C-43/95 *Data Delecta Aktiebolag and Ronny Forsberg v MSL Dynamics*.[25] The question there arose as to whether Article 6 of the EC Treaty precluded a Member State from requiring a legal person established in another Member State which had brought, before one of its courts, an action against one of its nationals or a company established in the Member State in question to lodge security for the costs of the proceedings, where no such requirement could be imposed on legal persons from that Member State. The Court ruled that national legislative provisions which fall within the scope of application of the Treaty are, by reason of their effects on intra-Community trade in goods and services, necessarily subject to the general principle of non-discrimination without any need to connect them with the specific provisions of Articles 30, 36, 59 and 66 of the Treaty. Although the national procedural rule in question was not intended to regulate activity of a commercial nature, it had the effect of placing traders not established in that Member State in a less advantageous position. It was therefore held that Article 6 EC precluded a Member State laying down such a requirement.

However, not every difference in national legislation amounts to discrimination. An example is Italian legislation which provided that a victim of a criminal offence wishing to bring an action as a civil party in criminal proceedings had to grant his representative a special power of attorney, when the law of the Member State of which the victim is a national did not lay down such a formality. The question arose as to whether this amounted to discrimination on the grounds of nationality. Reaffirming its consistent case-law, the Court ruled that in prohibiting every Member State from applying its law differently on the ground of nationality, within the

24. Case C-379/92 *Matteo Peralta* [1994] ECR I-3453.
25. [1996] ECR I-4661.

field of application of the Treaty, 'Articles 6, 52 and 59 are not concerned with any disparities in treatment which may result, between Member States, from differences existing between the laws of the various Member States, so long as they affect all persons subject to them in accordance with objective criteria and without regard to their nationality'.

It might be thought that the express prohibition of discrimination on the grounds of nationality set out in Article 6 is so wide as to preclude the development of any wider general principle. However, it is limited to discrimination on the grounds of nationality, and by its nature has tended to relate to the conduct of Member States, whereas, as will be evident from the other examples of the principle of non-discrimination discussed in this chapter, the Court has developed a general principle of equality of treatment, not limited to nationality, which is binding on the Community institutions themselves. So, for example, in Case C-37/89 *Weiser v Caisse Nationale des Barreaux Français*,[26] the Court described the principle of equal treatment as a 'fundamental right' which is binding on the Community institutions. The case involved a provision of the EC Staff Regulations on pension rights which differentiated between officials who had been in employment before they were recruited, whose pension rights could be transferred, and those who had been self-employed, whose rights could not be transferred. The Court found that this was a difference in treatment which was not justified by the difference in circumstances, and held the provision to be invalid.

Tax discrimination

In the context of the taxation of goods, it may be observed that Article 95 of the Treaty expressly prohibits discrimination in this area with regard to goods imported from other Member States. Two distinct requirements are contained in the first two paragraphs of Article 95 of the EC Treaty. The first paragraph states that 'no Member State shall impose, directly or indirectly, on the products of other Member States any internal taxation of any kind in excess of that imposed directly or indirectly on similar domestic products', and the second states that 'no Member State shall impose on the products of other Member States any internal taxation

26. [1990] ECR I-2395.

of such a nature as to afford indirect protection to other products'. The difference between their consequences was noted at an early stage in Case 27/67 *Fink-Frucht v HZA München-Landsberger-strasse*,[27] where it was said that, while the first paragraph only prohibits taxation in so far as it exceeds a clearly defined level, the second paragraph is based on the protective effect of the taxation in question to the exclusion of any exact standard of reference. The ease or otherwise of the calculation will depend on how close the relationship is between the competing domestic and imported goods at issue.

Community law does not in principle prohibit domestic tax laws from imposing or permitting different rates of tax on different products or, indeed, on products which may serve similar economic ends.[28] What it does object to is differential taxation of similar or competing products where the category of goods paying the higher rate is composed largely or exclusively of imported goods. Examples may be given include the French taxation of cars on the basis of engine size,[29] the French distinction between grain-based spirits and fruit-based spirits,[30] and the Italian distinction between sparkling wine fermented in bottle and in cask.[31]

The question of general principles arises here because Article 95 is limited to imports and does not deal with the discriminatory taxation of exports. Nevertheless, the European Court has held that the principles underlying Article 95 may also be applied to exports,[32] i.e. internal taxation which discriminates against exports is regarded as being in breach of the Treaty. Since there is, however, an express provision with regard to charges equivalent to customs duties in Article 16, it might have been wondered whether that might be the appropriate measure to deal with fiscal discrimination against exports. However, with one exception, the European Court has also applied to exports its view that the same duty cannot both be equivalent to a customs duty and part of a scheme of internal taxation. The point first arose in Case 27/74 *Demag v HZA Duisburg-Sud*,[33] when Germany introduced a 'special turn-

---

27. [1968] ECR 223.
28. Case 21/79 *Commission v Italy* [1980] ECR 1.
29. Case 112/84 *Humblot* [1985] ECR 1367.
30. Case 168/78 *Commission v France* [1980] ECR 347.
31. Case 278/83 *Commission v Italy* [1985] ECR 2503.
32. Case 142/77 *Statenskontrol v Larsen* [1978] ECR 1543.
33. [1974] ECR 1307.

over tax' on exports, apparently in an attempt to reduce its balance of payments surplus with the rest of the Community. It was claimed that this was a charge equivalent to a customs duty on exports, but the Court repeated the need to distinguish such charges from internal taxation, and held that the German tax in fact fell within the system of internal taxation (it amounted to a removal of an exoneration from tax for exports), and therefore could not contravene Article 16.

The exception referred to above occurred when the Court held in a subsequent judgment[34] that the same charge on exports could both breach Article 16 and the principles underlying Article 95 – but at least it was the first time the possibility of a breach of those principles by a charge on exports had been recognised. The problem was finally resolved in Case 142/77 *Statenskontrol v Larsen*,[35] where it was said that the aim of the Treaty was to guarantee generally the neutrality of systems of internal taxation with regard to intra-Community trade whenever an economic transaction going beyond the frontiers of a Member State at the same time constituted the chargeable event giving rise to a fiscal charge within the context of such a system. It was therefore necessary, according to the Court, to interpret Article 95 as meaning that the rule against discrimination which forms the basis of that provision also applies when the export of a product constitutes such a chargeable event. The Court concluded that it would be incompatible with the structure of the tax provisions in the Treaty to allow Member States, in the absence of an express prohibition, to apply internal taxation in a discriminatory manner to products intended for export to other Member States. Here again, therefore, a legislative gap has been filled by the Court and a general principle of non-discrimination with regard to goods traded between Member States has been created.

However, it is also in the context of taxation that the EC Treaty contains a provision apparently allowing differential treatment. Article 73d(1)(a), which entered into force on 1 January 1994 at the beginning of the second stage of Economic and Monetary Union, provides that in the context of free movement of capital and payments, the prohibition of restrictions on capital movements and payments is without prejudice to the right of Member

---

34. Case 51/74 *Hulst v Produktschap voor Siergewassen* [1975] ECR 79.
35. [1978] ECR 1543.

States to apply provisions of their tax law which distinguish between taxpayers who are not in the same situation with regard to their place of residence or with regard to the place where their capital is invested. It may be wondered how this provision may be reconciled with the concept of a single market for financial services, and, more particularly, how it may be reconciled with the principle of non-discrimination underlying the Treaty provisions on free movement of persons and provision of services. The most straightforward approach would be to argue that it is only concerned with monetary movements as such[36] and that it does not apply to situations governed by the other Treaty freedoms. Such an approach, however, does not appear to take account of Article 52 (second paragraph) or Article 61(2) of the Treaty. These provisions were not altered by the Single European Act or by the Maastricht Treaty. The second paragraph of Article 52 defines freedom of establishment as including the right to take up and pursue activities as self-employed persons, and to set up and manage undertakings, 'subject to the provisions of the Chapter relating to capital', and Article 61(2) states that the liberalisation of banking and insurance services connected with movements of capital shall be effected in step with the progressive liberalisation of the movement of capital. This link between the Treaty rules on establishment and the provision of services and the rules relating to the movement of money was noted in the recitals to the Second Banking Directive, which recognise that capital safeguard measures under the 1988 Capital Movements Directive[37] may lead to restrictions on the provision of banking services. The provision of banking and insurance services therefore appears expressly to be subordinated to the rules on monetary movements. More generally, the provisions of Article 73b, and therefore the exception in Article 73d(1)(a), relate not only to capital movements as such but also to payments, which, as 'current payments' under the old Article 106(1) were defined in terms of payments or transfers relating to the exercise of the other Treaty freedoms. Indeed, it may be wondered how far payments and transfers can be separated from the substantive Treaty freedom: in Case 95/81 *Commission v*

---

36. See Vanistendael, 'The consequences of *Schumacker* and *Wielockx*: two steps forward in the tax procession of Echternach' (1996) 33 CMLR 255; and Wattel, 'The EC Court's attempts to reconcile the Treaty freedoms with international tax law' (1996) 33 CMLR 223.
37. Council Directive 88/361 (OJ 1988 L178/5).

Italy[38] an import deposit scheme imposed in the context of exchange control legislation was classified as a measure equivalent to a quantitative restriction on the import of goods.

While it is beyond the scope of this book to discuss the case-law in this area in any detail, it has been clearly held in the context of the Treaty freedoms that the fact that a taxpayer is non-resident does not necessarily justify a difference in treatment. In the context of services, in Case C-80/94 *Wielockx v Inspecteur der Directe Belastingen*[39] the Court, while accepting that in principle the situations of residents and non-residents are not generally comparable, held that a non-resident taxpayer who receives all or almost all his income in the State where he works is objectively in the same situation as concerns income tax as a resident of that State. Similarly, in the context of freedom of establishment, in Case C-330/91 *R v Inland Revenue Commissioners, ex p Commerzbank*,[40] it was held that a German company which traded in the United Kingdom through a branch established there but which was fiscally non-resident in the United Kingdom, was entitled to receive interest on the repayment of tax which should not have been charged to it, if an undertaking resident in the United Kingdom would have received interest on such a repayment – and it made no difference that the only reason for the repayment of the tax was the fact that the German company was not resident in the United Kingdom.

With regard to free movement of workers, in Case C-279/93 *Schumacker*[41] and Case C-151/94 *Commission v Luxembourg*[42] it was made clear that discrimination cannot be justified where the taxpayer benefits from the rules on free movement of workers, and in Case C-107/94 *Asscher*,[43] it was made clear that discrimination cannot be justified where the taxpayer benefits from the rules on freedom of establishment. In the first case it was held that where the State of residence could not take account of the taxpayer's personal and family circumstances because the tax payable there was insufficient to enable it to do so, the Community principle of equal treatment required that in the State of employment the personal and family circumstances of a foreign non-resident be taken into

38. [1982] ECR 2187.
39. [1995] ECR I-2493.
40. [1993] ECR I-4017.
41. [1995] ECR I-225.
42. [1995] ECR I-3685.
43. [1996] ECR I-3089.

account in the same way as those of resident nationals, and the same tax benefits should be granted. In the second case it was held that it was a breach of the rules on the free movement of workers for Luxembourg to retain and not repay excess amounts of tax deducted from the earnings of Community nationals who resided or worked in Luxembourg for less than the whole tax year, and in the third case, the Netherlands could not impose a higher income tax liability on a non-resident to compensate for the fact that he paid social security contributions in another Member State.

It is therefore clear that there is a conflict between the Treaty rights of freedom of establishment and free movement of workers as interpreted in *Commerzbank*, *Wielockx*, *Schumacker*, *Luxembourg* and *Asscher*, and the discriminatory tax treatment apparently authorised by Article 73d(1)(a). However, Article 73d(1)(a) only entered into force on 1 January 1994, and there is attached to the Maastricht Treaty a Declaration in the following terms:

> The Conference affirms that the right of Member States to apply the relevant provisions of their tax law as referred to in Article 73d(1)(a) of this Treaty will apply only with respect to the relevant provisions which exist at the end of 1993. However, this Declaration shall apply only to capital movements between Member States and to payments effected between Member States.

While a mere Declaration may not amend the terms of the Treaty, it has long been established in other areas of Community law that it may be binding upon its author.[44] If the Member States are bound by their Declaration, it may be submitted that its effect is that with regard to monetary movements between Member States, the only discriminatory measures which may be maintained under Article 73d(1)(a) are those which were lawfully in force at the end of 1993. Since the *Commerzbank*, *Wielockx*, *Schumacker* and *Asscher* cases all relate to situations arising before the end of 1993, it may be suggested that the discrimination on the basis of residence found unlawful in those cases cannot be revived under Article 73d(1)(a).

---

[44]. In the context of Declarations under Regulation 1408/71 on social security, see Case 35/77 *Beerens* [1977] ECR 2249 at p. 2254.

Gender discrimination

The original version of the EC Treaty dealt with gender discrimination only in Article 119 with regard to equal pay for equal work as between men and women, although this will be altered when the Treaty of Amsterdam 1997 enters into force. The 1997 amendments introduce a new paragraph 3 providing also for measures with regard to equal opportunities and equal treatment in matters of employment and occupation in general. However, while the 1976 judgment in *Defrenne No. 2*[45] may be justly renowned for having established, at least prospectively, the direct effect of the principle of equal pay for equal work enounced in Article 119 of the EEC Treaty, it is sometimes forgotten that a much wider concept of equality between the sexes had already been recognised by the European Court in the exercise of its jurisdiction to determine disputes between officials of the Community and their employing institution (a jurisdiction which in 1989 was transferred to the European Court of First Instance). Thus, in 1972 it was held in *Sabbatini v European Parliament*,[46] in the context of the payment of expatriation allowances, that 'the Staff Regulations cannot ... treat officials differently according to whether they are male or female, since termination of the status of expatriate must be dependant for both male and female officials on uniform criteria, irrespective of sex'. The provisions of the Staff Regulations at issue in that case effectively provided that an official became 'head of household' as a result of the marriage, a concept normally referring to a married male official, and only including a married female official in the case of invalidity or serious illness of the husband; the Court in fact stated that a decision depriving a female official of the allowance on the basis of these provisions was 'devoid of any legal basis'. In the result, the Staff Regulations were amended so as both to delete the provisions relating to the loss of expatriation allowance on marriage and to delete the concept of 'head of household'.

Then, in 1975, the Court was faced with the problems of a female official who acquired her husband's nationality on marriage; in *Airola v Commission*[47] a Belgian female official working at the Euratom Research Centre at Ispra in Italy had her expatriation allowance withdrawn by the Commission when she married an

Italian and by Italian law acquired Italian nationality, thus ceasing, in the Commission's view, to be an 'expatriate'. After noting that under no national legislation would a male official acquire the nationality of his wife, the Court stated that the concept of nationality in this concept must be interpreted 'in such a way as to avoid any unwarranted difference of treatment as between male and female officials who are, in fact, placed in comparable situations' and must therefore be defined as excluding nationality imposed by law; hence equality of treatment required that Mrs. Airola continued to be an expatriate despite her marriage.

In 1984, however, there came a milestone in the development of equal rights for men. In cases 75a and 117/82 *Razzouk and Beydouin v Commission*,[48] the Court – and it may be noted that although this was a staff case, it was decided by the Full Court and not by a Chamber – held that in principle the widower of an official should have the same pension rights as the widow of an official. Under the provisions of the Staff Regulations at issue, the widow of an official could receive her pension irrespective of her dependency on her husband and her own resources, whereas the widower of a deceased official could receive a pension only if he had no income of his own and could show that he was permanently incapacitated by invalidity or serious illness from engaging in gainful employment, and even then his pension would be lower than that paid to a widow. The Court referred to its judgments in *Sabbatini* and *Airola*, and also in *Defrenne No 3*[49] as authority for the proposition that equal treatment of the sexes is one of the fundamental rights whose observance the Court has a duty to ensure, and therefore concluded that it must annul the Commission's decision to refuse Mr. Razzouk's request for a widower's pension as being based on provisions of the Staff Regulations which breached a fundamental right and were therefore not to be applied in so far as they treated surviving spouses of officials differently according to their sex. The Court further declared that it was for the Community institutions to take the necessary consequential legislative measures, but that in the meantime the applicant's claim for a pension should be dealt with on the basis of the provisions relating to widows.

Important as this decision may be, it could hardly be claimed that the European Court was breaking new ground. The US Su-

48. [1984] ECR 1509.
49. [1978] ECR 1365.

preme Court had already held in *Califano v Goldfarb*[50] that a 'gender-based' dependency requirement for widowers (i.e. widowers had to show dependency on their wives for one-half of their support in order to obtain 'spousal benefits') violated the equal protection component of the Due Process Clause of the Fifth Amendment. It may, however, be observed that the consequence of that judgment was an amendment to the US Social Security Act which, while repealing the dependency requirement for widowers, introduced offset provisions requiring the reduction of 'spousal benefits' by the amount of Federal or State government pensions received by the claimant, so that in practice most widowers would receive no benefit from the repeal of the dependency requirement. Transitional provisions were, however, introduced to exempt from the offset requirement those eligible for a pension before the end of 1982 who would have been entitled to unreduced benefits under the legislation as administered in January 1977 before the decision in *Califano v Goldfarb*, including therefore dependant widowers, and in *Heckler v Matthews*[51] these transitional provisions were upheld, despite the resurrection of a 'gender-based' dependency test, on the basis that they were 'related to the important governmental interest of protecting individuals who planned their retirements in reasonable reliance on the law in effect prior to that decision'. Fortunately, the provisions of the EC Staff Regulations dealing with survivors' pensions were amended so as to allow widowers to be treated the same way as widowers rather than so as to include a general set-off provision.

Of wider legal interest in *Razzouk* is its reference to Article 119 of the EEC Treaty as merely a very limited application of the general principle of equality of treatment, despite its popularity in the United Kingdom as a method of remedying the deficiencies of our the United Kingdom's equal pay legislation. In *Defrenne No. 3*[52] the Court had expressly held that Article 119 could not be interpreted as prescribing, in addition to equal pay, equality in respect of other working conditions applicable to men and women, and while recognising that the elimination of discrimination based on sex forms part of the fundamental rights whose observance the Court has a duty to ensure, the Court pointed out that as between

[50.] 97 S Ct 1021 (1977).
[51.] 104 S Ct 1387 (1984).
[52.] [1978] ECR 1365.

employer and employee, where their relationship was governed by national law, the Community had not at the relevant time assumed any responsibility for guaranteeing that principle with regard to working conditions other than remuneration. However, in *Razzouk* it was affirmed that as between Community institutions and their officials, and those claiming through such officials, the requirements of the general principle of equality of treatment were in no way limited to those issuing from Article 119 of the Treaty or Community directives adopted in this area: thus, it would appear that the general principle itself may control the activities of the Community authorities, and that the role of Article 119 and the Directives is to act as a legal mechanism to apply specific aspects of the general principle to those who are not directly subject to the general principles of Community law as such. It may also be wondered whether questions might be raised as to the compatibility with this general principle of Article 7 of Council Directive 79/7 of 19 December 1978 on equal treatment for men and women in matters of social security, which allowed the determination of different pensionable ages for men and women and was uncritically accepted by the Court in *Burton v British Railways Board*.[53] It may simply be observed that the Court subsequently held the age of retirement to be a condition of employment falling within the terms of Council Directive 76/207 on equal treatment as regards access to employment, vocational training and promotion, and working conditions in Case 152/84 *Marshall v Southampton Area Health Authority*,[54] and that occupational pensions were held to be 'pay' within the meaning of Article 119 in Case C-262/88 *Barber v Guardian Royal Exchange Assurance Group*.[55]

Following this, however, it has been held that a survivor's pension provided for by an occupational pension scheme may fall within the scope of Article 119,[56] and in this context the principle of *Razzouk* has in fact been applied at the national level. In Case C-147/95 *Dimosia Epicheirisi Ilectrismou (DEI) v Evthimios Evrenopoulos*[57] it was held that, to the extent that a survivor's pension fell within the scope of Article 119, Article 119 precluded the application of a provision of national law which made the award

---

[53] [1982] ECR 555 at p. 576.
[54] [1986] ECR 723.
[55] [1990] ECR I-1889.
[56] Case C-109/91 *Ten Oever* [1993] ECR I-4879.
[57] 17 April 1997.

of such a pension to a widower subject to special conditions which were not applied to widows. It was further held that (as in *Razzouk*, but without expressly mentioning that decision) widowers discriminated against in breach of Article 119 should be awarded a pension or other survivor's benefit under the same conditions as widows.

However, the principle will not be applied at the national level to situations not governed by Community law. Thus, in Case C-228/94 *Atkins v Wrekin District Council*,[58] where a 63-year-old man was refused concessionary fares on public transport and brought an action alleging discrimination on the grounds of sex, as he would have qualified for concessions if he had been a woman, the European Court held that concessionary fares did not fall within the scope of the Directive 79/7 on the progressive implementation of the principle of equal treatment for men and women in matters of social security, and it did not employ the general principle of non-discrimination.

It is also the case that Directive 76/207 on equal treatment of men and women with regard to conditions of employment has been held not to justify positive discrimination on an automatic basis. In Case C-450/93 *Kalanke v Freie Handsestadt Bremen*,[59] Mr. Kalanke considered himself to be unfairly discriminated against in that a woman, Ms. Glissmann, who was equally qualified for the position as Section Manager in the Bremen Parks Department was recommended for the position before him solely on the grounds of national legislation under which women with the same qualifications as men were given priority in occupations in which women were under-represented (deemed to be the case where women do not make up at least half of the staff in the individual pay brackets in the relevant personnel group).

Following the opinion of A. G. Tesauro, the Court ruled that the exception to the general principle of equal treatment (as implemented in terms of Article 2(1) of Directive 76/207 stating that 'there shall be no discrimination on the grounds of sex either directly or indirectly') in Article 2(4) of that Directive, which provides that the Directive 'shall be without prejudice to measures to promote equal opportunity for men and women, in particular by removing existing inequalities which affect women's opportunities',

---

58. [1996] ECR I-3633.
59. [1995] ECR I-3051.

was not intended to sanction national legislation such as the German provision in question. In the view of the Court, national rules which guarantee woman absolute and unconditional priority for appointment or promotion go beyond promoting equal opportunities and overstep the limits of the exception in Article 2(4) of the Directive. In *Kalanke* the Court was of the opinion that Article 2(4) of the Directive had to be interpreted strictly, as it embodied a derogation from an individual right laid down in the Directive. In any event, positive discrimination does not lie comfortably within the general principle of equality, as A. G. Tesauro explained in his Opinion. However, the Social Protocol agreed at Maastricht between all the Member States other than the United Kingdom permits certain national legislation which discriminates positively in favour of women, and the version of Article 119 resulting from the Treaty of Amsterdam provides in its paragraph 4 that 'the principle of equal treatment shall not prevent any Member State from maintaining or adopting measures providing for specific advantages in order to make it easier for the under-represented sex to pursue a vocational activity or to prevent or compensate for disadvantages in professional careers'. Furthermore, it is now clear that the decisions in *Kalanke* itself only relates to situations where women are *automatically* given preference. In Case C-409/95 *Marshall v. Land Nordrhein Westfalen*[59a] the European Court of Justice accepted that a slightly different national rule giving preference to women was not incompatible with the 1976 Directive. Under the rule in question, where male and female candidates were equally qualified, and there were fewer women than men at the relevant level of employment, priority was to be given to the promotion of female candidates unless reasons specific to an individual male candidate tilted the balance in his favour. This was held not to be incompatible with the Directive provided there was an objective assessment of the criteria, and the criteria did not discriminate against the female candidates.

However, the general principle of equality of treatment has been used to interpret the equal treatment legislation so as to apply to transsexuals. Case C-13/94 *P v S and Cornwall County Council*[60] involved a claim for unfair dismissal on the grounds of sex when P was given notice after informing his superior that he was

---

[59a.] 11 November 1997.
[60.] [1996] ECR I-2143.

to undergo a sex change. A. G. Tesauro commented upon the ever wider recognition of transexuality by the Member States, and by the Commission and Court of Human Rights in relation to the European Convention on Human Rights. He emphasised the fact that the law must keep up with contemporary moral and societal standards. He then went on to say that he regarded as obsolete the idea that the law should take into consideration, and protect, a woman who has suffered discrimination in comparison with a man, or vice versa, but deny that protection to those who are discriminated against, again by reason of sex, merely because they fall outside the traditional man/woman classification. In his view, ' ... the prohibition of discrimination on the grounds of sex is an aspect of the principle of equality .... What matters is that, in like situations, individuals should be treated alike'.

The Court in its judgment broadly followed A. G. Tesauro's Opinion, holding that Article 5(1) of Directive 76/207 was simply an expression of the general principle of equality, which is one of the fundamental principles of Community law. Article 5 therefore precluded P's dismissal as it constituted discrimination on the grounds of sex.

Agriculture

Article 40(3) of the EC Treaty provides expressly that common organisations 'shall exclude any discrimination between producers or consumers within the Community'. As interpreted by the European Court in Case 5/73 *Balkan v HZA Berlin-Packhof*,[61] this refers to discrimination as between producers or as between consumers, the relationship between the two groups being the concern of Article 39 of the EEC Treaty, stating the objectives of the Common Agricultural Policy. Discussion of the precise scope of this provision, and, in particular, of the question whether it produces direct effects has, however, been overtaken by the fact that the Court has held that it is, as in the other areas of Community law discussed above, 'merely a specific enunciation of the general principle of equality which is one of the fundamental principles of Community law'.[62] On the other hand, there are a number of deci-

---

61. [1973] ECR 1091 at p. 113.
62. Cases 117/76 and 16/77 *Ruckdeschel v HZA Hamburg-St Annen* [1977] ECR 1753 at p. 1769; Cases 124/76 and 20/77 *Moulins Pont à Mousson v ONIC* [1977] ECR 1795 at p. 181.

sions holding that, in the particular circumstances, differences in treatment do not amount to discrimination, or are objectively justified. Examples which might be given are Case 8/78 *Milac v HZA Freiburg*,[63] where the Court found that, on the material before it, the plaintiff had not shown what constituted the discrimination alleged to result from provisions applying a corrective amount to imports into Germany and the Benelux countries from other Member States of skimmed-milk powder but not to imports of whole-milk powder, and Case 2/77 *Hoffmann's Stärkefabriken v HZA Bielefeld*,[64] where the Court held that there were objective grounds for the difference between the treatment accorded potato-starch producers and that accorded maize-starch producers by Regulations reducing the production refund on maize-starch and potato-starch but allowing special transitional measures with regard to potato-starch alone.

The fine dividing line between valid and invalid differences in treatment imposed upon another subgroup of starch producers, the manufacturers of isoglucose, is illustrated in Cases 103 and 145/77 *Royal Scholten Honig v Intervention Board*,[65] in which isoglucose manufacturers challenged the validity of Council Regulations respectively freezing and eventually eliminating production refunds on maize-starch (and other agricultural starches) used for the manufacture of isoglucose, and introducing a system of production levies on the manufacture of isoglucose. With regard to the Regulation freezing and eliminating the production refund, the Court repeated that Article 40(3) was a specific enunciation of the principle of equality, which 'requires that similar situations shall not be treated differently unless the differentiation is objectively justified'. In the light of this, the Court went on to consider whether the situation of isoglucose was comparable to that of other products of the starch industry – and it is, in the light of the reference in Article 40(3) to 'producers', in itself interesting to note that it was the products rather than the producers which the Court considered. It was found that there was no competition between starch and isoglucose, or between isoglucose and other products derived from starch, except possibly glucose, and that even there the two products had different applications so that they could not be in a comparable competitive situation. On the other hand, it

---

63. [1978] ECR 1721.
64. [1977] ECR 1375.
65. [1978] ECR 2037.

was stated that as isoglucose was at least partially interchangeable with sugar, the maintenance of the production refund in favour of manufacturers of isoglucose might have constituted discrimination against manufacturers of sugar. From this, although it had referred initially to the general principle of equality, the Court concluded that the Regulation did not infringe the rule of non-discrimination between Community producers set out in the second sub-paragraph of Article 40(3) of the Treaty.

In relation to the introduction of a production levy on isoglucose, the Court considered whether isoglucose and sugar were in comparable situations. It pointed out that the Council had recognised in the recitals to the Regulation that isoglucose was a direct substitute for liquid sugar, and, in the recitals to a Regulation amending that Regulation, that 'any Community decision on one of those products necessarily affects the other'. Having found that isoglucose and sugar were, in effect, in a comparable position, the Court went on to state that isoglucose manufacturers and sugar manufacturers were, nevertheless, treated differently as regards the imposition of the production levy, in that it only affected sugar produced outside the basic quota but within the maximum one, whereas it applied to the whole of isoglucose production. It was also noted that sugar manufacturers benefited from the intervention system, whereas isoglucose manufacturers did not. The final question, however, was whether this difference in treatment could be objectively justified. On behalf of the Council and Commission, it was argued that, since the price of isoglucose tended to follow the intervention price of sugar, the high intervention price of sugar (stated to be 15 per cent higher than the price which would have been fixed by normal criteria) gave a notional 15 per cent advantage to isoglucose, which roughly corresponded to the five units of account maximum levy. The Court rejected this argument, stating that a similar advantage, if it existed, could be enjoyed by a sugar manufacturer with a favourably situated modern factory.

It was, further, argued that the levy roughly corresponded to the charges borne by sugar manufacturers on the whole of their production, if that produced outside the quotas was taken into account. The Court rejected this argument also, pointing out that sugar manufacturers paid beet growers a reduced price for beet used for sugar produced outside the basic quota, and that sugar manufacturers could limit their charges simply by limiting their production – in effect, keeping to their quotas – whereas a limit on production by an isoglucose manufacturer would be without effect as regards the rate of levy per unit of weight. The Court held, although this time it had commenced simply by a reference to Article 40(3) of the Treaty, that the provisions of the Regulation establishing the production levy system for isoglucose offended against the general principle of equality of which the prohibition on discrimination set out in Article 40(3) of the Treaty was a specific expression.

The isoglucose cases show very clearly the Court's methodology when dealing with an alleged breach of the principle of equality. The first step is to see whether the products or producers between which or whom there is said to be discrimination are, in fact, in a comparable situation, which in the cases discussed above appears to have been synonymous with a competing position. If they are not, as was the case with isoglucose and other starch products, that is the end of the matter. If they are in a comparable situation, the next step is to see if there is a difference in treatment between them. If there is a difference in treatment, the third and final step is to see whether it is objectively justified – and the approach of the Court in the isoglucose cases appears to have been that it was for the institutions to show that the difference was objectively justified rather than for the producers affected to show that it was not justified.

A fairly straightforward example of discrimination may be found in Case C-309/89 *Codorniu v Council*.[66] The action concerned a provision in a Council Regulation[67] which reserved the word 'crémant' for certain quality sparkling wines produced in specified regions of France and Luxembourg. According to the recitals, the aim was to protect traditional descriptions used in France and Luxembourg. The applicant was a Spanish company manufacturing quality sparkling wines produced in specified regions, and it had since 1924 designated one of its wines 'Gran Cremant de Codorniu', a graphic trade mark of which it was the holder. The Regulation prevented it using the term 'crémant' in relation to Spanish wines and thus from using its trade mark, so the applicant sought its annulment. It was held on the substance that the reservation of the word 'crémant' to France and Luxembourg treated comparable situations differently and could not be justified

---

[66] [1994] ECR I-1853.
[67] Council Regulation 2045/89 (OJ 1989 L202/12).

on objective criteria, so that the provision constituted discrimination contrary to Articles [6] and 40(3) of the EC Treaty.

Although, at first sight, Article 40(3) and the underlying general principle may seem only to govern the validity of Community legislation, the European Court has held in Cases 201 and 202/85 *Klensch v Luxembourg Secretary of State for Agriculture*[68] that it applies to any measure taken in the context of a common organisation of an agricultural market, whether that measure is taken by the Community authorities or the national authorities. Hence, in that case, the exercise by the Luxembourg government of its discretion under the milk-quota system to choose the reference year from which quotas would be calculated was held to be subject to the principle of non-discrimination.

Furthermore, the general principle of equality of treatment is applied not just to producers and consumers in the Community but also, for example, to importers, as in Case 165/84 *Krohn*,[69] where it was held that the principle was breached by legislation which did not allow importers of manioc from Thailand to cancel their licences, following the introduction of a quota regime, but did allow such licences to be cancelled by those importing manioc from any other country. This was reaffirmed with regard to the market in bananas (which are largely imported into the Community from third countries) in Case C-280/93 *Germany v Council*.[70] It was there stated that 'the common organisation of the market for the banana sector covers operators who are neither producers nor consumers. However, because of the general nature of the principle of non-discrimination, the prohibition of discrimination also applies to other categories of economic operators who are subject to the common organisation of a market'. The Court then went on to dismiss the plea of breach of the principle on the grounds that the situations of the different economic operators were not comparable due to the different market systems operated by the Member State prior to the adoption of the Regulation at issue, and the differences in treatment introduced by the Regulation were essentially inherent in the objective of integrating previously compartmentalised markets.

---

68. [1986] ECR 3477.
69. [1985] ECR 3997.
70. [1994] ECR I-4973.

CHAPTER THREE

Proportionality

Definitions and scope

It has been said that 'proportionality embodies a basic concept of fairness which has strengthened the protection of individual rights at both the national and the supranational level',[1] but the same author has also admitted that 'it is difficult to describe in abstract terms the precise meaning and scope of the principle in question'.[2] Be that as it may, the concept has been invoked in numerous cases before the European Court and has been expressly incorporated into the text of the Treaty of Amsterdam 1997. What is, however, clear is that the concept is used in a number of different contexts in Community law, and that its content varies in emphasis depending on the context in which it is used.

At a simple level of classification, distinctions can be made between its use in the context of determining the competence or legislative capacity of the Community and its institutions, its use in relation to the legitimacy of the burdens imposed on those subject to Community law, and its use in assessing the conduct of Member States when they are acting within the scope of Community law.

The incorporation of the concept into the Treaty arises in the context of Community competence and legislative capacity in conjunction with the concept of subsidiarity.[3] The idea in fact underlies the definition of subsidiarity introduced as Article 3b of the EC Treaty by the Maastricht amendments; the last paragraph of Article 3b states that 'any action by the Community shall not go

---

1. Emiliou, *The Principle of Proportionality in European Law* (Kluwer, 1996) p. 1.
2. Ibid. p. 2.
3. See the papers by Toth, Steiner and Emiliou in O'Keeffe and Twomey (eds), *Legal Issues of the Maastricht Treaty* (Chichester, 1994) at pp. 37, 49 and 65.

beyond what is necessary to achieve the objectives of this Treaty'. In the Protocol on the application of the principles of subsidiarity and proportionality added by the Treaty of Amsterdam, it is stated that in exercising the powers conferred on it, each institution shall ensure that the principle of subsidiarity is complied with, and that it shall also ensure compliance with the principle of proportionality, 'according to which any action by the Community shall not go beyond what is necessary to achieve the objectives of the Treaty'. In other words, what was already in Article 3b is stated to be the definition of proportionality, with the emphasis very much on the question whether a Community institution should act in the first place rather than on the consequences of what it has done.

An example of this aspect of the concept of proportionality may be found in C-359/92 *Germany v Council*,[4] where Germany claimed that Article 9 of Council Directive 92/59 on general product safety was void on the grounds of breach of the principle of proportionality in so far as it empowered the Commission to adopt, with regard to a particular product, a decision requiring Member States to take measures among those listed in Article 6(1)(d)–(h) of the Directive. Germany argued that the Commission's powers were not appropriate, as there was no guarantee that the measures required to be taken would be the most suitable, and it also argued the same objective could be attained by recourse to the infringement procedure under Article 169 of the EC Treaty. The Court observed that it had consistently held that the principle of proportionality required that measures taken by the Community institutions should be appropriate to achieve the objective pursued without going beyond what is necessary to that end. With regard to the specific arguments of the German government, the Court held, first, that the difficulties which might arise if the appropriate measures are determined on a case-by-case basis led to the conclusion that the powers conferred upon the Commission are not inappropriate for the achievement of a high level of consumer protection, and secondly, that Article 169 proceedings did not permit the same results as the exercise of the powers set out in Article 9 of the Directive, since under Article 169 proceedings no obligation could be placed on Member States to take a specified measure from among those listed in Article 6(1)(d)-(h) of the Directive and, in particular, the infringement procedure would not en-

4. [1994] ECR I-3681.

able consumer protection to be secured in the shortest possible time.

However, the case-law doctrine of proportionality with which that term is most usually associated, and which falls into the second of the classifications given above, is concerned rather more with the consequences of the actions of a Community institution rather than with the question whether it should have acted at all. A brief definition was clearly stated in Case C-66/82 *Fromançais:*[5] 'In order to establish whether a provision of Community law is consistent with the principle of proportionality it is necessary to establish, in the first place, whether the means it employs to achieve the aim corresponds to the importance of the aim and, in the second place, whether they are necessary for its achievement.' Clearly, here the assessment is of the means used rather than of the need to act, and a more detailed version was given in Case C-331/88 *R v Minister for Agriculture, Fisheries and Food, ex p FEDESA and others.*[6] This involved a reference for a preliminary ruling as to the validity of Council Directive 88/146 prohibiting the use in livestock farming of certain substances having hormonal action. The Ministry of Agriculture, Fisheries and Food claimed that the measure was inappropriate, unnecessary and that it entailed excessive disadvantages, in particular considerable financial losses suffered by the traders concerned, in relation to the alleged benefits accruing to the general interest. The European Court there stated that it had 'consistently held that the principle of proportionality is one of the general principles of Community law. By virtue of that principle, the lawfulness of the prohibition of an economic activity is subject to the condition that the prohibitory measures are appropriate and necessary in order to achieve the objectives legitimately pursued by the legislation in question; when there is a choice between several measures recourse must be had to the least onerous, and the disadvantages caused must not be disproportionate to the aims pursued'.

However, the Court also made it clear in that judgment that the Community may be justified in imposing even substantial negative financial consequences for certain traders where the importance of the objectives pursued is such as to justify it. Furthermore, with regard to the question of judicial review,[7] the Court emphasised that,

---

5. [1983] ECR 395 at p. 404.
6. [1990] ECR I-4203.
7. See Chapter 8 below.

in matters concerning the common agricultural policy, the Community legislature enjoyed a discretionary power, so that the legality of a measure adopted in that sphere could be affected only if the measure was manifestly inappropriate having regard to the objective which the competent institution was seeking to pursue.

Finally, with regard to the assessment of the conduct of Member States when they are acting within the scope of Community law, the question of proportionality largely arises in the context of national measures which may in principle be permissible under Community law but which have the effect of limiting or restricting the exercise of the Treaty freedoms. A number of examples will be considered at the end of this chapter, but a comprehensive summary of the application of the principle of proportionality in this area was given in Case C-55/94 *Gebhard*.[8] The European Court there stated that national measures liable to hinder or make less attractive the exercise of fundamental freedoms guaranteed by the Treaty 'must be suitable for securing the attainment of the objective which they pursue' and 'they must not go beyond what is necessary in order to attain it'. Here, therefore, the essential point is the appropriateness of the restriction on the exercise of the Community freedom.

Despite these differences in emphasis, it may be suggested that a common feature is a determination of the necessity for or appropriateness of the measure at issue. This is likely in its nature to involve a judicial assessment of policy issues, which perhaps explains the reluctance of judges in the United Kingdom to apply the concept in domestic law.[9]

Development of the case-law concept

The principle of proportionality first made its appearance in Community law at a time when that term referred only to the Coal and Steel Community, in the judgment of the Court in Case 8/55 *Fédération Charbonnière de Belgique v High Authority*.[10] In this case, the applicants had argued that rather than fix Belgian coal prices by general decision, the High Authority could ensure that

8. [1995] ECR I-4165.
9. See Chapter 9 below.
10. [1954 to 1956] ECR 245 at p. 299.

such prices reached the desired level by withdrawing compensation payments (intended to compensate for the high cost of coal production in Belgium) from those enterprises which did not make a sufficient reduction in price. The Court, however, rejected this proposition and stated that 'in application of a generally accepted rule of law', action of the High Authority in response to a wrongful act of an enterprise must be proportionate to the gravity of that act. In the context, this might not seem to say more than the truism that the punishment must fit the crime, and indeed the principle has often been invoked in cases where the High Authority or Commission has imposed a fine.[11] However, it is in the sense defined by A. G. Dutheillet de Lamothe in his Opinion in Case 11/70 *Internationale Handelsgesellschaft v Einfuhrund Vorratsstelle Getreide*[12] that the principle has its real importance in Community law: 'citizens may only have imposed on them, for the purposes of the public interest, obligations which are strictly necessary for those purposes to be attained.'

In this sense, it is the Germans who have a word for it, 'Verhältnismässigkeitsgrundsatz', which has been held to be the principle underlying Articles 2 and 12 of the Basic Law, laying down certain basic freedoms and the limits within which they may be exercised, even though no specific mention is made of the principle.[13] It is interesting to read the views of M. Dutheillet de Lamothe on this matter;[14] after mentioning the existence of the rule in Germany, he stated that the legality of a Community measure can never be judged in the light of national law but that fundamental principles of national legal systems 'contribute to forming that philosophical, political and legal substratum common to the Member States from which through the case-law an unwritten Community law emerges', and he concluded, referring to the earlier case-law, that the principle of 'proportionality' was already guaranteed by the general principles of Community law.

The Court in its judgment also emphasised that the validity of a Community measure or its effect within a Member State cannot be determined with reference to the legal rules or concepts of national

---

11. See Case 8/56 *ALMA v High Authority* [1957 and 1958] ECR 95 at p. 100; Case 7/72 *Boehringer v Commission* [1972] ECR 1281 at p. 1290.
12. [1970] ECR 1125 at p. 1146; [1972] CMLR 255.
13. See cases cited in Schmidt-Bleibtrau and Klein *Kommentar zum Grundgesetz* (Luchterhand, Neuwied, 6th edition 1983) at pp. 171 and 294.
14. [1970] ECR at pp. 1146–7.

law as such.[15] To do so would deprive the measure of its character as Community law. However, it stated that an examination should be made as to whether or not 'any analogous guarantee inherent in Community law' had been disregarded, pointing out that respect for fundamental rights formed an integral part of the 'general principles of law' protected by the Court. It further asserted that while the protection of such rights might be inspired by the constitutional traditions common to the Member States, it had to be ensured within the framework of the structure and objectives of the Community. Having said all this, the European Court then found that the system of export deposits at issue in this case did not breach the Community law principle of proportionality – and it is of interest to observe that, in parallel proceedings before the German Constitutional Court, that court reached the same conclusion applying the principle of proportionality as a principle of German law (even if in so doing it took a different view as to the status of fundamental rights entrenched on the German constitution).[16]

A further illustration of the Court's use of the principle of proportionality is to be found in Cases 114, 116, 119–120/76 *Bela-Mühle etc.*,[17] a series of references for preliminary rulings. The Court there held that Council Regulation No. 563/76, effectively requiring manufacturers of animal foodstuffs to incorporate intervention skimmed-milk powder into their products at a price *three times* that of the soya husks for which it was substituted, imposed an obligation which was disproportionate, and not necessary to attain the objective of reducing stocks of milk powder (and discriminatory within the meaning of Article 40(3)(2) of the EEC Treaty). Not surprisingly, it held the Regulation to be invalid, although in a related action for damages, it was found that the harm suffered by the producers did not exceed the risks inherent in their trade.[18]

In more recent case-law, the principle has been used to emphasise the difference between primary and secondary obligations, so that while the forfeiture of a large security may not be disproportionate in relation to a failure to perform the primary obligation to carry out the export transaction, it is disproportionate in relation to a marginal failure to comply with a secondary obligation to

15. At p. 1134.
16. For an English-language version of the judgment see [1974] 2 CMLR 540.
17. [1977] ECR 1211.
18. Cases 83 and 94/76, 4, 15 and 40/77 *Bayerische HNL v Council* [1978] ECR 1209. See Chapter 8 below.

apply for an export licence within a fixed time limit, at least where that need not prevent the export transaction being carried out. This situation arose in Case 181/84 *E.D. and F. Man v Intervention Board*,[19] where it was held that if the objective of a deposit was to ensure that sugar was exported it was a breach of the principle of proportionality to require the forfeiture of the whole deposit when the exporter was late (by a few hours) in applying for the formal export licence, when there was still enough time to carry out the export transaction. The basis of this decision was a distinction between the primary obligation to carry out the export transaction and the secondary obligation to apply for an export licence within a specific time, the Court taking the view that to penalise failure to comply with the secondary obligation as severely as failure to comply with the primary obligation would breach the principle of proportionality. A further gloss was put on the distinction between primary and secondary obligations in Case 21/85 *Maas v Bundesanstalt für Landwirtschaftliche Marktordnung*,[20] where a deposit paid under the food-aid legislation had been forfeited because the exporter loaded the goods into ships a few days late and because the ships used were older than the 15 years specified in the legislation. The Court held the obligation to load the goods within a fixed time-limit was a primary obligation, but that in the context of sea transport a delay of a few days did not necessarily breach that obligation, and, since the goods, in fact, arrived at their destination on time, the loss of the deposit could not be justified. With regard to the use of ships less than 15 years old, which was held not to be a primary obligation, particularly since it was not required under other similar legislation, it was decided that this requirement should be interpreted as including ships equated with ships less than 15 years old for insurance purposes, and that even if the ships used did not fall within the requirement as so interpreted, it was disproportionate to require the whole deposit to be forfeited.

A possible overlap between the principles of proportionality and non-discrimination was noted in Cases 114, 116, 119–120/76 *Bela-Mühle etc.*,[21] mentioned above, in so far as the Community legislation failed to take account of the differences between the

19. [1985] ECR 2889.
20. [1986] ECR 3537.
21. [1977] ECR 1211.

producers concerned. There are, however, examples where such situations have been considered simply in the light of the principle of proportionality. In one group of cases[22] three Commission Regulations were held invalid on the grounds of violation of the principle of proportionality because excessively high 'additional amounts' were levied on imports of preserved mushrooms, which did not distinguish between preserved mushrooms of different origins and grades, thereby increasing the cost of imported preserved mushrooms, particularly those of lower quality. Hence, the Regulations in question penalised imports of lower quality mushrooms to a greater extent.

The issue arose again[23] in relation to the validity of Council Regulation No. 1796/81 (which was enacted as a replacement of the three Commission Regulations declared invalid in the cases mentioned above). This time, the Court held that the Council and the Commission had infringed the principle of proportionality by setting a charge levied on imports of preserved mushrooms at an excessively high level. The Court noted that, when applying the principle of proportionality, measures imposing financial charges on economic operators were lawful provided that they were appropriate and necessary for meeting the objectives legitimately pursued by the rules in question. However, when there was a choice between several appropriate measures, the least onerous measure must be used and the charges imposed must not be disproportionate to the aims pursued. Rejecting the Commission's arguments, the Court noted that the Regulation was substantially the same as those previously annulled and concluded that a flat-rate charge which was set at a very high level and was levied on all traders who exceeded the quantities prescribed – regardless of whether they did so inadvertently or fraudulently – was excessive, because it went beyond the objective of the Regulation, which was to protect the Community market, and penalised importers. Consequently, the principle of proportionality had been infringed.

---

22. Case C-21/90 *Werner Faust* [1991] ECR I-4905; and Joined Cases C-25/90 and C-26/90 *Wünsche Handelsgesellschaft* [1991] ECR I-4939 and I-4961.
23. Case C-296/94 *Bernhard Pietsch v Hauptzollamt Hamburg-Waltershof* [1996] ECR I-3409 and Case C-295/94 *Hüpeden & Co. KG v Hauptzollamt Hamburg-Jonas* [1996] ECR I-3375.

Limits on the principle

While the principle of proportionality may be frequently invoked, there are many judgments of the Court upholding the letter of technical requirements or accepting that the burdens placed on traders were justified. An example is the decision in Case 9/85 *Nordbutter*[24] in the context of legislation granting a subsidy on skimmed-milk used for feeding animals other than calves. This required a quarterly declaration of the number of calves on the holding, and under Commission Regulation 188/83 the subsidy was reduced by 10 per cent if the declaration was up to 10 days late, and was lost totally thereafter. It was held by the Court that, since this expressly allowed for minor infringements of the deadline, it did not breach the principle of proportionality.

On the other hand, technical definitions may be strictly interpreted, so that to require grapes to be turned into must and the must into wine in the immediate vicinity of the region concerned, in order for a wine to qualify as a quality wine produced in a specified region (VQPRD), was held to be necessary, in order to achieve the objectives of the legislation and, therefore, not to breach the principle of proportionality.[25] Similarly, quality standards for food aid have been strictly enforced. In Case C-326/94 *A. Maas & Co. NV v Belgische Dienst voor Bedrijflsleven en Landbouw*[26] a question arose as to the interpretation of Commission Regulation 1824/80 opening an invitation to tender for the mobilisation of common wheat as food-aid for the Republic of Benin. The Court ruled that the principle of proportionality was not violated by the forfeiture of a security, even where the successful tenderer for a Community contract committed only a very minor infringement of the quality standards stipulated. The Court stated that the importance of such a condition, which it treated as a principal obligation of the tenderer, could not be underestimated, either as regards the inherent requirements of food-aid or as regards equality of conditions (i.e. non-discrimination) as between tenderers.

Highly technical rules laid down for the payment of, for example, denaturing premiums may well be strictly applied. Case

---

24. [1986] ECR 2831.
25. Case 116/82 *Commission v Germany* [1986] ECR 2519.
26. [1996] ECR I-2643.

272/81 *Ru-mi v FORMA*[27] involved a highly specific formula for the denaturing of skimmed-milk powder so as to ensure it could not be used as a feed for young calves, the intention being that it could, however, be used as feed for pigs and poultry. The Court took the view that it was not disproportionate to withhold the whole of the special aid for denaturing if the formula was not strictly followed, because of the risk that the product might thereby be diverted from its intended use. On the other hand, Council Regulation 1300/84[28] introduced a legislative application of the principle of proportionality in the context of premiums for the non-marketing of milk and the conversion of dairy herds, so that a reduced premium could be paid where there were minor breaches of the rules, rather than the premium being entirely lost.

In Case C-8/89 *Zardi*[29] legislation providing for a levy to be collected from cereal producers when cereals were placed on the market, which would be reimbursed only if production did not exceed the Maximum Guaranteed Quantity (MGQ) for the given year, was challenged on the grounds of proportionality. It was claimed that less restrictive means could have been employed, and, in particular, that the levy should not have to be paid before the MGQ had actually been exceeded. The Court held that the Community legislature had not committed any manifest error of assessment in rejecting other options as collection of the levy at the time when the cereals were placed on the market was likely to persuade the producers not to increase production during the marketing year. It also accepted that it was more cost-effective than a system of securities or guarantees. A similar view was taken of the MGQ system in the tobacco market in Cases C-133, C-300 and C-362/93 *Crispoltoni*.[30] The Court held that, as the MGQs fixed in previous years had not been exceeded for the majority of the varieties of tobacco at issue, it could not be argued that the system at issue was manifestly inappropriate for the objective pursued. Furthermore, and of more general relevance, it was stated that the mere fact that the system had proved insufficiently effective was not enough to justify the conclusion that the Regulation was invalid.

27. [1982] ECR 4167.
28. OJ 1984 L125/3.
29. [1990] ECR I-2515.
30. [1994] ECR I-4863.

The proportionality of the conduct of the Member States

The concept of proportionality has been used as a test to determine the legitimacy of the actions of Member States in a wide range of areas governed by Community law.[31] However, its substantive importance my be illustrated by taking the example national measures falling within the scope of the Community provisions on the free movement of goods. The earliest mention of the principle of proportionality in this area was in fact in legislation rather than case-law. Article 33(7) of the EC Treaty gave the Commission original power to issue Directives establishing the procedure and timetable for the abolition of measures equivalent to quantitative restrictions. Under this power, the Commission issued Directive 70/50[32] which, although it must be read subject to the directly effective terms of Article 30 itself,[33] remains of interest both as a catalogue of certain types of prohibited conduct and as an illustration of the Commission's attitude at the time of its enactment.

Its most substantial provision is Article 2, which relates to measures other than those applicable equally to domestic or imported products, i.e. those which are discriminatory in their nature.[34] Equally applicable measures as such are mentioned only in Article 3 of the Directive, which prohibits measures governing the marketing of products which deal, in particular, with shape, size, weight, composition, presentation, identification or putting up and which are equally applicable to domestic and imported products but only where the restrictive effect of such measures on the free movement of goods exceeds the effects intrinsic to trade rules, in particular where the restrictive effects on the free movement of are *out of proportion* (emphasis added) to their purpose or where the same objective can be attained by other means which are less of a hindrance to trade. In principle, therefore, equally applicable trading rules only breach Article 3 of the Directive if they have disproportionately restrictive effects on imports. It should be said at once

---

[31.] See the examples given in Chapter 8 below.

[32.] OJ 1970 L13/29.

[33.] See Opinion of A.G. Warner in Case 12/74 *Commission v Germany* [1975] ECR 181 at p. 208.

[34.] For a fuller discussion see Green, Hartley and Usher, *The Legal Foundations of the Single European Market* (Oxford, 1991) Chapter 6.

that this is not the approach followed by the European Court; rather than holding equally applicable trading rules to be prohibited only if they produce disproportionately restrictive effects on trade, its *Cassis de Dijon*[35] case-law rests on the basis that an equally applicable national trading rule which hinders the import of a good lawfully sold in another Member State is prohibited unless it may be justified as protecting a 'mandatory requirement' or under the terms of Article 36 of the Treaty, and the question of proportionality or reasonableness goes to its justification as a mandatory requirement[36] or as a measure falling under Article 36.[37] The example may be given of Case 261/81 *Rau*[38] which involved Belgian legislation requiring margarine to be packed in cubic blocks, allegedly to enable purchasers to distinguish it from butter, thus preventing the importation of oblong blocks or round tubs from other Member States. Clearly, this involved shape and presentation as mentioned in Article 3 of the Directive, but rather than looking at the proportionality of the restriction as such, the Court looked to see if it could be justified as a mandatory requirement (in this case to protect consumers) and considered whether the restriction was proportionate in that context (holding that it was not).

On the other hand, before its judgment in Cases C-267 and 268/91 *Keck*,[39] the Court used to apply a proportionality test to see whether a measure might be regarded as breaching Article 30 in those cases where the measure itself was not regarded as being connected with importation or exportation. To take the example of Case 145/88 *Torfaen Borough Council v B & Q plc*,[40] where the Sunday trading rules in England were at issue, it was first stated that such rules reflected certain political and economic choices and were not designed to govern the patterns of trade between the Member States. The Court then went on to refer expressly to Article 3 of the Directive in order to hold that the rules would not breach Article 30 of the Treaty unless their restrictive effects exceeded what was necessary to achieve the aim in view and exceeded the effects intrinsic to trade rules. However, in its

---

[35]. Case 120/78 *Rewe v Bundesmonopolverwaltung für Branntwein* [1979] ECR 649.
[36]. See e.g. Case 788/79 *Gilli* [1980] ECR 2071.
[37]. See e.g. Case 124/81 *Commission v United Kingdom* [1983] ECR 203.
[38]. [1982] ECR 3961.
[39]. [1993] ECR I-6097.
[40]. [1989] ECR 3851.

judgment in *Keck*, the Court made a distinction between rules relating to goods themselves (e.g. as to designation, form, size, weight, composition, presentation, labelling, packaging) which would breach Article 30 if they constituted obstacles to the free movement of goods, unless their application could be justified by a public interest objective, and national provisions restricting or prohibiting certain selling arrangements within the Member State, which were not to be regarded as hindering trade between Member States provided they were non-discriminatory both in law and in fact.

Proportionality remains of relevance, however, with regard to mandatory requirements, as mentioned above, and with regard to the restrictions permitted under Article 36 of the EC Treaty. Taking the example of the protection of the health and life of humans, animals or plants under that provision, the issues of necessity, reasonableness and proportionality arose in the context of the protection of human health in Case 104/75 *De Peijper*.[41] Under Dutch legislation, certain information had to be supplied to the relevant authorities before pharmaceutical products could be marketed, and this information was of a type which could only be supplied by the manufacturer (or, in practice, an importer authorised by the manufacturer). The accused was prosecuted for marketing products in the Netherlands, which had been bought in the United Kingdom, without supplying the requisite information to the Dutch authorities. Those products were very similar, if not identical, to products already marketed in the Netherlands by the same manufacturer or an authorised importer, and with regard to which the relevant information had already been supplied. It was first held that rules which mean that only traders authorised by the manufacturer may effect imports in principle breach Article 30, and in this context the Court thought it particularly important that parallel imports should not be placed at a disadvantage, since they are usually lower priced, and 'the effective protection of health and life of humans also demands that medicinal preparations should be sold at reasonable prices'. However, while recognising that 'health and life of humans rank first among the property or interests protected by Article 36', the Court held that restrictive measures are compatible with the Treaty only to the extent to which they are necessary for the effective protection of health and life of humans. Measures are not necessary if health and life could be protected by

---

41. [1976] ECR 613.

other measures which restrict trade to a lesser extent; in particular Article 36 cannot justify practices explained primarily by a concern to lighten the burden on the administration or reduce public expenditure, unless this burden or expenditure would otherwise clearly exceed the limits of what could reasonably be required.

In the light of these general considerations, the Court held it was not necessary for a second trader who imported a medicinal preparation in every respect the same as one with regard to which the necessary information had already been given by another trader to supply that information again. With regard to the conformity of individual batches with the general information already received, it was held that a trader could not be required to produce documents to which he did not have access, when national authorities could require manufacturers or their agents to produce information, or they could cooperate with the authorities of other Member States. It might finally be observed that the reasonableness test in *De Peijper* relates not just to the burden on the trader but also to the burden on the public authorities; it therefore requires a balancing of those considerations.

Perhaps the clearest example of import controls being regarded as disproportionate is Case 124/81 *Commission v United Kingdom*,[42] which concerned the United Kingdom rules on the importation of UHT milk. These rules contained two main elements. The first was a requirement to obtain an import licence, which in principle has long been held to breach Article 30,[43] claimed by the United Kingdom to be necessary in effect to police health requirements. The Court held this to be disproportionately restrictive, suggesting that the objectives in question could be attained by, for example, requiring declarations from importers, accompanied if necessary by the appropriate certificates. The second element was that UHT milk should be packed in a dairy approved by the competent local authority, i.e. that it should be packed in premises within the United Kingdom. In practice, this meant that the milk had to be retreated in the United Kingdom, since the original packs could not be opened without losing the benefits of the UHT treatment. Retreatment would make importation uneconomic, so the requirement amounted to a total prohibition on imports. In the view of the Court, the United Kingdom could protect the health of

---

42. [1983] ECR 203.
43. Cases 51 & 54/71 *International Fruit v Produktschap voor Groenten en Fruit* [1971] ECR 1116.

consumers by a requirement that importers produce certificates issued by the competent authorities of the exporting Member States,
coupled with controls by means of samples.[44]

The dividing-line between sampling and systematic analysis has
been a matter of some debate. It has been held to be disproportionate for the French authorities to analyse three out of four consignments of Italian wine, in the absence of evidence of fraud or
irregularities;[45] such action was also found to be discriminatory in
view of the fact that no similar practice existed in relation to
French wine. In an order for interim measures in that case,[46] the
Court ordered that analyses should be restricted to a maximum of
15 per cent of the consignments. On the other hand, in Case 37/83
Rewe-Zentrale v Landwirtschaftskammer Rheinland,[47] inspection
of up to one in three consignments was held to be valid as sampling; such a level of inspections was in fact laid down in a Directive,[48] and the question at issue was whether the provisions of the
Directive contravened the principles of Articles 30 and 36. The
view taken by the Court was that the Council had not exceeded
the limits of its discretion, although the very incomplete nature of
the harmonisation effected by the Directive was emphasised. This
also serves to show that the questions of the legitimacy of national
actions and the legitimacy of Community actions may not be entirely separate issues.

As indicated at the beginning of this chapter, the approach developed in particular (though not exclusively) in the context of the
free movement of goods has now been generalised, notably in the
declaration in Case C-55/94 *Gebhard*,[49] which was concerned with
the dividing line between freedom of establishment and freedom to
provide services, that national measures liable to hinder or make
less attractive the exercise of fundamental freedoms guaranteed by
the Treaty 'must be suitable for securing the attainment of the objective which they pursue' and 'must not go beyond what is necessary in order to attain it'.

---

44. The matter of UHT milk has subsequently been regulated by Council Directive
85/397 (OJ 1985 L226/13) on health and animal-health problems affecting
intra-Community trade in heat-treated milk.
45. Case 42/82 *Commission v France* [1983] ECR 1013.
46. Case 42/82R, [1982] ECR 841.
47. [1984] ECR 1229.
48. Council Directive 77/93 (OJ 1977 L26/20) on protective measures against the
introduction into the Member States of harmful organisms of plants or plant
products.
49. [1995] ECR I-4165.

CHAPTER FOUR

Legitimate expectations and legal certainty

General issues

In so far as it may be relied upon statistically, a trawl of the LEXIS database in August 1997 indicated that the phrase 'legal certainty' had been invoked in more than 900 cases before the European Court (compared with over 700 citations of 'proportionality' and over 500 citations of 'legitimate expectation' or 'legitimate confidence'). It may be suggested that this both shows its practical importance in Community law, and betrays the fact that it is in reality an overarching concept within which fall such concepts as the protection of legitimate expectation and the principle of non-retroactivity. Although this latter principle will not be considered separately in this chapter, 'legal certainty' cases involving retroactivity illustrate the interrelationship. Thus, in Case 88/76 *Exportation des Sucres v Commission*,[1] the Court held that the principle of legal certainty precluded a Community measure from taking effect from a time before its publication. However, despite similar linguistic overlap, a certain element of retroactivity was accepted in Case C-108/81 *Amylum v Council*.[2] Amylum sought the annulment of Regulation 387/81, reproducing the provisions of Regulation 1293/79, which in turn had been declared void by the Court in a preceding case.[3] Regulation 387/81 was to come into force retrospectively so as to apply as from the date in 1979 when Regulation 1293/79 had come into force. Amylum argued that this retroactive effect breached the general principle of legal certainty. The Court held that Amylum and other isoglucose producers had

---

1. [1977] ECR 709.
2. [1982] ECR 3107.
3. Case 138/79 *Roquette Frères v Council* [1980] ECR 3333.

no legitimate expectations worthy of protection, since they should have anticipated the imposition of restrictions upon the isoglucose market; in particular, it stated that since Regulation 1293/79 had been declared void on the grounds of a procedural irregularity (albeit the rather important one of failure to consult the European Parliament) it should have been clear that the substantive purpose and policy behind the provision would be reproduced.

The extent to which retroactivity may be justifiable was discussed in Joined Cases C-260/91 and C-261/91 *Diverinste SA v Administration Principal de Aquanas e Impuestos Especiales de la Junquera*,[4] again in conjunction with the concepts of legal certainty and legitimate expectation. The case involved the validity of a Commission Regulation dated 16 March 1987 which applied a charge to the export of certain milk products from Spain with effect from 12 February 1987. The Court ruled that, although as a general rule the principle of legal certainty precludes a Community act from taking effect from a date prior to its publication, it may exceptionally be otherwise where the purpose to be achieved requires it and where the legitimate expectation of those concerned is duly protected. However, although retroactive effect of Community decisions is not necessarily precluded, the Court emphasised that decisions having such effect must set out a justification for the desired retroactive effect in their statement of reasons (required by Article 190 of the EC Treaty[5]). In this case, the statement of reasons merely stated that, in order to prevent speculation, the Regulation's provisions should be introduced as a matter of urgency. As the Court indicated, that might explain the immediate application of the Regulation, but did not make it possible to review whether the retroactive effect was justified, or whether the legitimate expectation of the traders in question was protected. The Regulation was therefore held invalid.

On the other hand, it might finally be observed in this context that it is clear that retroactive application of Community legislation will be regarded as permissible where the legislation at issue leads to a more favourable legal situation for those affected to the extent that their legitimate expectation is duly respected.[6]

---

4. [1993] ECR I-1885.
5. See Chapter 7 below.
6. Case C-310/95 *Road Air BV v Inspecteur der Invoerrechten en Accijnzen* (22 April 1997).

Legitimate expectation

Development of the Community concept

Like the principle of proportionality, the principle of the protection of legitimate expectation is widely regarded as being related to a German concept, in this case 'Vertrauensschutz'. This is another principle held by the German courts to underlie certain provisions of the Basic Law, notably Article 2.[7] The equivalent French term used in Community law is 'protection de la confiance légitime', which was originally translated into English as 'protection of legitimate confidence', but it was thought that the technical meaning of 'confidence' in English law made this misleading, and the term 'expectation' was thought to be more appropriate and has become common parlance – as is explained in the Opinion of A.G. Warner in Case 4/75 *Einfuhr und Vorratsstelle Getreide v Mackprang*.[8]

This principle has not always been clearly distinguished from the general concept of legal certainty, as indicated above, or indeed from the French one of 'droits acquis' or established rights, as is evidenced by the following extract from Case 1/73 *Westzucker v Einfuhr und Vorratsstelle Zucker*:[9] 'It is asked .... whether the Regulation ... infringes a principle of legal certainty by which the confidence of persons concerned deserves to be protected ... It seems difficult to consider the amendment of a provision which was capable, because of its inflexibility, of causing losses or gains for those concerned, as adversely affecting any established position which they hold.' Again, the German court which made the order for reference mentioned the concept of 'Vertrauensschutz', but in his Opinion, A.G. Roemer specifically mentioned the fact that similar concepts, i.e. the principle that there must be no infringement upon 'well-established' rights, can also be found in French and Belgian case-law.[10] It was held, in fact, that the Regulation in question[11] did not infringe any such principle, even though it affected advance fixing certificates for the export of sugar issued before it entered into force, in so far as the importation had not yet taken place, by providing for an optional adjustment of the export

---

7. See cases cited in Schmidt-Bleibtrau and Klein, *Kommentar zum Grundgesetz* (Luchterhand, Neuwied, 6th edition 1983).
8. [1975] ECR 607 at p. 622.
9. [1973] ECR 723 at pp. 729–30.
10. [1973] ECR 723 at p. 739.

refund following alterations in the intervention price instead of the previous automatic adjustments.

However, the rule has been applied, as a general principle of Community law, in circumstances where it is difficult to say that any established rights were affected and where what was protected was purely and simply an 'expectation'. The prime example is the judgment of the Court in Case 81/72 *Commission v Council*,[12] where it was necessary to decide whether a Decision taken by the Council on 21 March 1972 to apply for a period of three years a particular system of adjusting the salaries of Community staff had a binding effect so as to prevent the Council from validly adopting a Regulation[13] which was not in accordance with its terms. In the words of the judgment:

> Taking account of the particular employer-staff relationship … the rule of protection of the confidence that the staff could have that the authorities would respect undertakings of this nature, implies that the Decision of 21st March 1972 binds the Council in its future action. Whilst this rule is primarily applicable to individual decisions, the possibility cannot by any means be excluded that it should relate, when appropriate, to the exercise of more general powers.

It is noteworthy that the Court, in so deciding, did not follow the Opinion of A.G. Warner[14] citing case-law in the Member States, and in particular English and French authorities, to the effect that such policy statements did not produce any binding obligation. It is therefore of particular interest to observe that it has now been accepted, even in English administrative law, that a course of conduct followed by an administrative authority may give rise to expectations which prevail over the strict legal position.[15]

It was in the context of the protection of legitimate expectation that the Court held that breach of a general principle could be a ground for annulment under Article 173 of the EC Treaty.[16] In Case 112/77 *Töpfer v Commission*[17] it was stated that 'the submission that there has been a breach of this principle is admissible

---

12. [1973] ECR 575 at p. 584.
13. Council Regulation 2647/72 (OJ 1972 L283/1).
14. [1973] ECR 575 at pp. 592–5.
15. *Council of Civil Service Unions v Minister for the Civil Service* [1984] 3 All ER 935. See Chapter 9 below.
16. See Chapter 8 below.
17. [1978] ECR 1019.

in the context of proceedings instituted under Article 173, since the principle in question forms part of the Community legal order with the result that any failure to comply with it is an 'infringement of this Treaty or of any rule of law relating to its application within the meaning of the article quoted'. However, the submission was not upheld in that case. The principle has also frequently been invoked as the basis for claims for damages against the Community institutions, and in particular it has been decided that a Community institution can be liable for harm caused by an act infringing this principle (by failing to allow a transitional period before abolishing a system of compensatory amounts) even where the legality of the act itself is not in question.[18] The applicant in the case in question claimed that the withdrawal by Commission Regulation No. 189/72[19] of the compensatory amounts applicable to colza and rape seeds violated the principle of legal certainty in that it had retroactive effect and in that it ignored the legitimate expectation of persons concerned that compensatory amounts would be maintained for current transactions. The Court decided that the Regulation did not have retroactive effect in the strict sense[20] and so considered the question of legitimate expectation. It was held that although the system of compensatory amounts could not be considered as a guarantee for traders against the risks of changes in exchange rates, their application in practice avoided the exchange risk.[21] Therefore even a prudent trader might be induced to omit to cover himself against such risk.[22]

A limitation was, however, imposed on the applicant's right to recover in that 'the protection which it may claim by reason of its legitimate expectation is merely that of not suffering loss by reason of the withdrawal of those amounts', since the maintenance of the system was in no way guaranteed and the applicant could not legitimately expect under all circumstances to make the profits which would have accrued under the previous system.

It appears however that expectations may only be based upon situations which already exist or upon what are termed precise

---

18. Case 74/74 *CNTA v Commission* [1975] ECR 533.
19. OJ 1972 L24/25.
20. [1975] ECR 533 at p. 458.
21. Under the original system which applied at the relevant time, monetary compensatory amounts covered the difference between official parities and real value of a national currency in terms of the dollar.
22. [1973] ECR 533 at pp. 549–50.

assurances. In Case T-571/93 *Lefebvre and others v Commission*[23] the applicants claimed that their expectations were founded upon two letters from the Commission informing them that it would take into account the particular situation of small and medium-sized importers when it came to formulate a proposal for the Council for the establishment of a Community system in the banana sector. The Court of First Instance rejected the applicants' argument on the basis that there was an important difference between a statement made by the Commission in general terms, which could not engender any valid expectations, and an assurance in precise terms on which expectations might legitimately be based.

The exercise of discretion

It will be evident from the examples above that the exercise of legislative and administrative discretion may be subject to severe constraints in situations where a legitimate expectation has been created. A striking (and expensive) example relates to the milk-quota scheme. A series of actions were brought by dairy producers who had agreed to give up dairy production for a period of five years under an earlier Community scheme and had not produced any milk during the year (1983 in their case) taken as the base year for calculating the milk-quotas when the milk-quota system was introduced. They had therefore not been granted any milk-quota when the quota system was introduced in 1984 by Council Regulation 857/84. This meant in practical terms that they could not return to milk production when the five-year period expired. However, the Court held this legislation unlawful[24] as constituting a breach of the general principle of the protection of legitimate expectation. While it accepted that producer who had voluntarily ceased production for a certain period could not expect not to be subject to rules of market or structural policy adopted in the interim, nevertheless a producer who had been encouraged by a Community measure to suspend marketing for a limited period might legitimately expect not to be subject to restrictions which affect him only because he took advantage of the Community provisions. In particular, the Court held that they could not have foreseen that they would be totally excluded from the market.

23. [1995] ECR II-2385.
24. Case 120/86 *Mulder* [1988] ECR 2321; Case 170/86 *Deetzen* [1988] ECR 2355.

Following these judgments, the producers concerned were subsequently granted a quota based on 60 per cent of their production during the year before they began to take part in the 'outgoers' scheme by Council Regulation 764/89, and this also was held to be unlawful by the Court as a breach of the general principle of the protection of legitimate expectation.[25] This time, while accepting that it was legitimate to ensure that the outgoers did not gain an undue advantage by comparison with the producers who continued to deliver, it was found that the reduction applied to the outgoers was more than double the highest reduction suffered by producers who continued to deliver, so that again it was a restriction which affected the outgoers only because they took advantage of the Community provisions.

That an expectation limiting the exercise of legislative discretion may arise from reliance on rules not yet in force is shown in the decision of the Court of First Instance in Case T-115/94 *Opel Austria v Council*.[26] It was there held that once the Community had deposited its instruments of approval of the European Economic Area Agreement and the date of its entry into force was known, a trader was entitled, as a corollary to the principle of good faith in public international law, to form the legitimate expectation that the Community would not introduce measures affecting it in the intervening period contrary to the terms of the European Economic Area Agreement. Such an expectation was held to have been breached by the adoption of a Regulation on 20 December 1993 imposing duties on imports into the Community of the applicant's gearboxes, when the European Economic Area Agreement was due to come into force on 1 January 1994, and under that Agreement such duties were unlawful.

However, there is only a limit on the exercise of discretion where there is a legitimate expectation, and it has long been established that economic operators may not have a legitimate expectation that a situation which may be modified at the discretion of the Community institution will be maintained.[27] The European Court has asserted[28] that it has consistently held that, whilst the principle of the protection of legitimate expectations is one of the fun-

---

25. Case C-189/89 *Spagl* [1990] ECR I–4539; Case C-217/89 *Pastätter* [1990] ECR I-4585.
26. [1997] ECR II-39.
27. See e.g. Case C-350/88 *Delacre and others v Commission* [1990] ECR I-395.
28. Case C-353/92 *Greece v Council*[1994] ECR I–3411.

damental principles of the Community, traders cannot have legitimate expectations that an existing situation which is capable of being altered by the Community institutions in the exercise of their discretionary power will be maintained. This was said to be particularly true in an area such as the CAP and the organisation of the markets whose purpose involves constant adjustments to meet changes in the economic situation,[29] and the same view has been expressed with regard to anti-dumping legislation.[30]

Indeed, it may be recalled that, in the milk-quota cases discussed above, the expectation that was protected was not that the rules would remain unchanged when the outgoers returned to milk production, but that they should not be penalised compared with other producers for having participated in a Community scheme. The sorts of expectations which might be protected in these areas were indicated more generally in Case 97/76 *Merkur v Commission*,[31] in relation to the old system of monetary compensatory amounts.[32] It stated that, although the possibility of protecting the legitimate interests of the trader could not be excluded, the Community could, nevertheless, only be rendered liable for the damage suffered by such traders as a result of the adoption of legitimate measures governing the system of monetary compensatory amounts if, in the absence of any overriding public interest, the Commission were to abolish or modify the compensatory amounts applicable in a specific sector with immediate effect, and without warning, and in the absence of any appropriate transitional measures, and if such abolition or modification was not foreseeable by a prudent trader.

Knowledge and conduct of those concerned

It is settled case-law that the question whether the activity of the Community bodies is compatible with the principle of the protection of legitimate expectations must always be examined regard

---

29. See e.g. Case C-241/95 *R v Intervention Board, ex p Accrington Beef* [1996] ECR I-6699 at p. 6732.
30. Case T-155/94 *Climax Paper Converters v Council* [1996] ECR II-877 at p. 910.
31. [1977] ECR 1063.
32. See Usher, *Legal Aspects of Agriculture in the European Community* (Oxford, 1988) Chapter 5.

being had to the knowledge and information which is or should be available to the prudent and informed businessman.[33]

The fundamental point is that prudent traders are usually deemed to be familiar with the rules governing the sector in which they operate, and cannot have expectations which conflict with those rules. In Case 169/73 *Compagnie Continentale France v Council* [34] it was held that a Council resolution, published several months before the 1972 Accessions indicating what the accession compensatory amounts would be in trade with the United Kingdom, had to be read subject to the overall limitation in the Act of Accession that they were not to exceed the total amount levied by the relevant Member State on imports from third countries. Therefore, traders who knew the market could not simply rely on the resolution and ignore the Act of Accession.

Similarly, when the Spanish Act of Accession included a provision for a transitional period of seven years during which Spanish sugar prices should align with common Community prices, with a review after four years, and after the four-year period expired the Council introduced measures amending the price scheme with the result that the applicants were no longer going to receive Community aid, the Court held[35] that the applicants had no legitimate expectations that the aid would be continued because 'prudent and well-informed traders' ought to have realised that there might be early alignment of intervention prices.

A similar approach has also been applied to Community officials. In Cases T-33/89 and T-74/89 *Blackman v European Parliament*,[36] the applicant claimed that he had a legitimate expectation to have been informed by the appointing authority of the provisions for the interpretation of the term 'medical expenses' which would be reimbursed, adopted by the heads of administration in 1987; in his view this would have enabled him to take steps to prove that persons attending his daughter were legally authorised to practice a medical or paramedical profession and thereby to qualify for reimbursement of the costs of her remedial education. The Court of First Instance held, however, that while it was settled case-law that the right to rely on the principle of the protection of

---

33. Case C-350/88 *Delacre and others v Commission* [1990] ECR I-395.
34. [1975] ECR 117.
35. Case T-472/93 *Cambo Erbo Industrial SA v EU Council* [1995] ECR II-421.
36. [1993] II-ECR 249.

legitimate expectations extended to any individual who was in a situation in which it appeared that the conduct of the Community administration had led him to entertain reasonable expectations, an individual could not plead a breach of the principle unless the administration had given him specific assurances. In this case, it observed that the provisions for the interpretation of the insurance rules were 'public rules which were brought to the notice of and [were] accessible to the officials and servants of the Community institutions'. Therefore, the appointing authority's failure to draw his attention to those provisions could not have led him to hold a reasonable expectation that the cost of his daughter's remedial teaching programme would be reimbursed.

The situation was concisely summarised in Case T-2/93 *Air France v Commission*,[37] where the Court of First Instance stated that 'a Community institution cannot be forced, by virtue of the principle of the protection of legitimate expectations to apply Community rules *contra legem*'.

Exceptionally, however, the European Court may be willing to derogate from the principle that everyone is deemed to know the law. Although the case was not directly concerned with the principle of the protection of legitimate expectation, a rather different view was taken of the level of knowledge of traders in Greece following Accession in Case 160/84 *Oryzomyli Kavallas*,[38] where the facts that a Greek-language text of the relevant Community legislation was not available, that local civil servants had not received instructions in the matter, and that the relevant head of service was absent at the relevant time were found to constitute 'special circumstances' triggering the operation of Article 13 of Council Regulation 1430/79[39] allowing the remission of import and export duties in situations arising from special circumstances in which no negligence or deception may be attributed to the person concerned. With regard to the latter requirement, it was held that small undertakings far from Athens could not, in those circumstances, be expected to know the European Community rules for themselves.

Turning from a mere lack of knowledge to actual wrongful conduct on the part of those claiming to have formed a legitimate

---

37. [1994] ECR II-323.
38. [1986] ECR 1633.
39. OJ 1979 L175/1.

expectation, it has consistently been held[40] that the principle of the protection of legitimate expectations may not be relied upon by an undertaking which has committed a manifest infringement of the rules in force. Hence undertakings which had obtained a Community subsidy by declaring that they had paid more for new fishing vessels than was in fact the case could not claim that the effluxion of time between the grant of the aid and its withdrawal gave them any legitimate expectations.[41]

Who or what can create expectations?

It has frequently been stated that the principle of the protection of legitimate expectations may be invoked as against Community rules only to the extent that the Community itself has previously created a situation which can give rise to a legitimate expectation. By way of example,[42] where a group of dairy farmers were claiming special reference quantities (over and above their allotted milk-quotas) on the basis that they had adopted development plans under a Community Directive, which they had taken as a signal that they could produce more and a receive a special reference quantity, the Court held that there was nothing in the Directive which could allow producers to form a legitimate expectation that the adoption of a development plan would secure for them special treatment in relation to other producers, should measures to curb milk production be introduced.

A particular difficulty arises in relation to the power of individual officials to make representations which may be treated as the act of a Community institution. It was held in Case C-137/92P *Commission v BASF* [43] that a decision finding that an undertaking had breached Article 85 of the EC Treaty could not be the subject of a delegation of authority even to the Commissioner responsible for competition policy without offending against the principle of collegiality.

---

40. See e.g. Case 67/84 *Sideradria v Commission* [1985] ECR 3983; Cases T-551/93 and T-231-234/94 *Industrias Pesqueras Campos v Commission* [1996] ECR II-247 at p. 278.
41. Cases T-551/93 and T-231-234/94 *Industrias Pesqueras Campos v Commission* [1996] ECR II-247 at p. 278.
42. See e.g. Case C-63/93 *Duff and others v Minister for Agriculture and Food, Ireland, and the Attorney General* [1996] ECR I-576.
43. [1994] ECR I-2555.

It is also well established that no Community official can give a valid undertaking not to apply Community law,[44] and in one of the cases arising under the ECSC steel production quota system,[45] the Court held that the Commission is not bound by a statement of one of its senior officials promising that a fine will not be imposed; while that particular case also turned on the point that the Commission had no discretion but to impose a fine if a breach of the production quota was established, it appears to fall into the same category as the decision in a competition case,[46] holding that the view of a senior official that an agreement is capable of exemption could not bind the Commission.

On the other hand, in Cases 29, 31, 36, 39–47, 50 and 51/63 *Usines de la Providence v High Authority*,[47] where promises to pay a 'transport parity' were made consistently over a period of time by officials of the old ECSC High Authority, this was held to constitute a lack of care by the High Authority in supervising its officials, so that although the 'transport parities' as such could not be paid, the High Authority was liable in damages.

A further problem arises from the fact that most Community law is administered at the national level by national authorities and officials. At the least, it is clear that the conduct of a national authority which acts in breach of Community law, and has been declared by the Commission to be acting in breach of Community law, cannot give rise to a legitimate expectation. In Case C-24/95 *Land Rheinland-Pfalz v Alcan Deutschland*[48] it was held that the action of a regional government, which paid out a State aid without notifying the Commission under Article 93(3) of the EC Treaty, leading to a formal decision by the Commission holding the aid unlawful, could not create a legitimate expectation on the part of the recipient that the aid was legitimate. The recipient could not therefore resist a demand for repayment of the aid, even though the regional government waited so long before commencing proceedings for its recovery that the action would have been barred on grounds of legal certainty in German administrative law.

On the other hand, there are situations where Community law itself declares national authorities to be the competent authorities,

---

44. Case 188/82 *Thyssen v Commission* [1983] ECR 3721.
45. Cases 303 and 312/81 *Klöckner-Werke v Commission* [1983] ECR 1599.
46. Case 71/74 *FRUBO v Commission* [1975] ECR 563.
47. [1965] ECR 911.
48. [1997] ECR I-1591 at p. 1621.

and indeed specific provisions which protect legitimate expectations in this context. An example is Council Regulation 1697/79 on post-clearance recovery of import or export duties.[49] Article 5(2) of that Regulation provides for waiver of post-clearance recovery where the initial non-collection of the duty is due to an error by the competent authorities, the person liable has acted in good faith, and where that person has complied with all the legislative provisions in force with regard to the customs declaration. It has been held that 'competent authorities' in this context include 'any authority which, acting within the scope of its powers, furnishes information relevant to the recovery of customs duties and which may thus cause the person liable to entertain legitimate expectations'.[50] It has further been accepted that the competent authorities may, in an appropriate context, be the customs authorities of a country to which the EC Treaty does not apply, such as the Faroese authorities in Cases C-153 and 204/94 *R v Commissioners of Customs and Excise, ex p Faroe Seafood*.[51] It was there held that under the Commission Regulation defining 'originating products' for the application of the customs procedure for certain products coming from the Faroe Islands, it was for the Faroe Islands authorities to issue EUR.1 certificates if the goods could be regarded as originating there. The Court therefore concluded that the Faroese authorities were entrusted by the Community with the task of furnishing information relevant to the recovery of customs duties 'and may therefore arouse legitimate expectations in the person liable'.[52] This would be the case where the exporter had declared the goods to be of Faroese origin in reliance on the actual knowledge by the Faroese authorities of all the facts necessary for applying the customs rules in question. It would not, of course, be the case where those authorities had been misled by incorrect declarations on the part of the exporter, an illustration again of the fact that nobody can claim to rely on a situation caused by their own breach of Community law.

---

49. OJ 1979 L197/1.
50. Case C-348/89 *Mecanarte* [1991] ECR I-3277 at para. 22.
51. [1996] ECR I-2465.
52. Ibid. at p. 2541.

Legal certainty

It will have been noticed that protection of legitimate expectation is often associated with the broader concept of legal certainty. This is a principle so general that it cannot really be ascribed to any particular national source, yet it is of considerable importance in the case-law of the Court. However, given the large number of judgments in which the principle is cited, just two aspects of its current application, both of substantive importance, will be mentioned here.

The competition rules and direct effect

In the early 1970s, the European Court delivered its well-known decisions in the second *Brasserie de Haecht*[53] case and in *BRT v Sabam*[54] to the effect that Articles 85(1) and 86 of the EEC Treaty produce direct effects and could not therefore be modified or limited by Regulation No.17 of the Council.[55] This left, *inter alia*, problems as to the extent to which national courts could apply the notion of 'provisional validity' to agreements before them and as to possible conflicts of jurisdiction between national courts and the Commission. In relation to the former, the Court decided, in the *Brasserie de Haecht* case, that there was room for distinguishing agreements made before and after the implementation of Article 85 by Regulation No. 17, and that in the case of 'old' agreements, 'the general principle of contractual certainty requires, particularly when the agreement has been notified in accordance with the provisions of Regulation No. 17, that the court may only declare it to be automatically void after the Commission has taken a decision by virtue of that regulation'.[56]

The approach taken in the *Brasserie de Haecht* case with regard to 'old' agreements has been followed when the competition rules have been applied to new areas such as air transport, even though by then the basic principles of the EC competition rules can hardly have been unknown to economic operators. In Cases 209–213/84 *Ministère Public v Asjes*,[57] it was held that for reasons of legal

---

53. Case 48/72 *Brasserie de Haecht v Wilkin-Janssen* [1973] ECR 77.
54. Case 127/73 *BRT v SABAM* [1974] ECR 51.
55. OJ 1962 p. 204.
56. [1973] ECR 77 at pp. 86–7.
57. [1986] ECR 1425.

certainty the direct effect of Article 85 could not be invoked with regard to agreements relating to air transport before the enactment of secondary legislation applying the competition rules to that sector; on the other hand, the same view was not taken with regard to an alleged abuse of a dominant position under Article 86 in the air transport sector, in Case 66/86 *Ahmed Saeed*,[58] because there was no possibility of a negative clearance or an exemption being given in favour of such an abuse.

With regard to possible conflicts of jurisdiction between national courts and the Commission, it was held in the *SABAM* case that if the Commission initiates a procedure in application of Article 3 of Regulation No. 17, a national court may, if it considers it necessary for reasons of legal certainty, stay the proceedings before it while awaiting the outcome of the Commission's action.[59] However, it was said that the national court should continue to judgment if it decides either that the agreement or behaviour in dispute is clearly not capable of having any appreciable effect on competition or on trade between Member States, or that there is no doubt that the agreement or behaviour is incompatible with Article 85 or Article 86 of the EC Treaty.

The Court added further refinements to these requirements in Case C-234/89 *Delimitis v Henninger Bräu*,[60] where it suggested that if the national court considers, in the light of the Commission's rules and decision-making practices, that the agreement may be the subject of an exemption decision, or if it considers that there is a risk of conflicting decisions, it may decide to stay proceedings or adopt interim measures pursuant to its national rules of procedure. More generally, however, it was suggested that it is always open to a national court to seek information from the Commission as to the state of any procedure the Commission may have set in motion and as to the likelihood of its giving an official ruling on the agreement under Regulation No. 17. In particular, it was stated that the national court 'may contact the Commission where the concrete application of Article 85(1) and Article 86 raises particular difficulties, in order to obtain the economic and legal information which that institution can supply to it', given that, under Article 5, 'the Commission is bound by a duty of sincere cooperation' with the national judicial authorities.

58. [1989] ECR 803.
59. [1974] ECR 51 at p. 63.
60. [1991] ECR I-935.

This recognises the possibility of a kind of preliminary reference to the Commission, a matter taken up by the Commission itself in its Notice on Cooperation between national courts and the Commission in applying Articles 85 and 86.[61] The Commission there suggested that national courts could consult it on its 'customary practice' in relation to the Community law at issue, in particular with regard to the questions of the effect on trade between Member States and the extent to which the restrictions on competition resulting from the practices specified in Articles 85 and 86 may be regarded as appreciable. It emphasised, however, that it would not consider the merits of the case, that its answers would not be binding on the national courts that requested them, and that the right of the national court to make a reference to the European Court under Article 177 was not affected. The Commission nevertheless stated that it considered that its answers would give national courts useful guidance for resolving disputes.

Interesting as this concept may be, it may be suggested that, in so far as this approach is based on the concept of legal certainty, a national court faced with what might properly be categorised as a question as to the interpretation of EC competition law would find little advantage in obtaining a non-binding opinion from the Commission when it can obtain a definitive ruling from the European Court.

Temporal effects of judgments of the European Court

The other aspect of legal certainty which will be mentioned here relates to the temporal effects of the European Court's judgments. In the second *Defrenne* case,[62] the Court held that, although effect should have been given to Article 119 of the Treaty on equal pay in the original Member States from 1 January 1962, its direct effects could only be invoked from the date of the judgment (8 April 1976), on the grounds that, the conduct of the Commission and of certain Member States having led those affected to continue with practices which were contrary to Article 119, 'in these circumstances, it is appropriate to determine that, as the general level at which pay would have been fixed cannot be known, important considerations of legal certainty affecting all the interests involved,

---

61. OJ 1993 C39/6.
62. [1976] ECR 455.

both public and private, make it impossible in principle to reopen the question as regards the past'.

Leaving on one side the fact that this statement appears to imply that the mere conduct of the Commission may alter the effects of a Treaty provision which it could not alter by express legislation, it was this aspect of the decision in *Defrenne* which led Hamson[63] to comment that the development of the concept of direct effects had led the Court to claim and exercise a dispensing power not known to any modern court in any of the Member States 'in order to avoid mere chaos'. More recently, Hartley has stated that such a doctrine cannot be reconciled with legal principle.[64] On the other hand, it could be said to be an illustration of a restriction by a principle culled from national concepts on the scope of a power transferred to the Community. Be that as it may, the approach in *Defrenne* has been repeated, perhaps most famously in Case C-262/88 *Barber v Guardian Royal Exchange Assurance*[65] where, having held that a pension paid under a contracted-out private occupational scheme falls within the scope of Article 119 of the EEC Treaty, added that because of 'overriding considerations of legal certainty' the direct effect of Article 119 could not be relied upon in order to claim entitlement to a pension with effect from a date prior to that of the judgment unless proceedings had already been initiated or a claim already had been made. This appeared to leave, however, the possibility of claiming equal treatment after that date with regard to the payment of a pension arising from contributions made before that date, a possibility which led the Member States, in a Protocol to the Maastricht Treaty on European Union, to declare that 'for the purposes of Article 119 of this Treaty, benefits under occupational social security schemes shall not be considered as remuneration if and in so far as they are attributable to periods of employment prior to 17 May 1990' (the date of the *Barber* judgment) unless proceedings had been initiated or claims made before then. This in itself could have given rise to interesting questions as to the expectations or rights which might have arisen between the date of the judgment and the

---

63. Hamson, *Methods of interpretation – a critical assessment of the results*, Reports of the Judicial and Academic Conference (Luxembourg, 1976).
64. Hartley, 'The European Court, Judicial Objectivity and the Constitution of the European Union' (1996) 112 LQR 95.
65. [1990] ECR I-1889.

entry into force of the Maastricht Treaty, but in Case C-109/91 *Ten Oever*[66] the European court in fact found this to be the correct interpretation of its judgment in *Barber*.

A similar approach has been taken where the Court has changed its interpretation of Community legislation. In Case C-308/93 *Cabanis-Issarte*,[67] the Court broadened the interpretation it had maintained for the previous 20 years[68] as to certain rights of the spouses of migrant workers under Council Regulation 1408/71 on social security. Since it recognised that its judgment departed from its previous case-law, the Court held that for reasons of legal certainty, its judgment would in general only apply for the future: 'overriding consequences of legal certainty preclude legal situations being called into question which have been definitively settled in accordance with the Courts previous case law, whose scope is limited by this judgment. Accordingly, it must be held that this judgment cannot be relied on in support of claims concerning benefits relating to periods prior to the date of delivery of this judgment, except by persons who have, prior to that date, initiated proceedings or raised an equivalent claim.'

Similar problems arise in so far as the system of references for preliminary rulings on the validity of Community acts has enabled individual litigants, through their national courts, to bring before the European Court questions as to the validity of general Community legislation which they could not have challenged directly. It has thus happened that a private citizen who could not possibly have brought an action for annulment successfully challenged the validity of a provision of general legislation some fifteen years after its enactment[69] in Case 41/84 *Pinna v Caisse d'Allocations Familiales de la Savoie*.[70] The Court in fact there ordered that the invalidity of the provision at issue should only be invoked as from the date of its judgment, except as regards those who had already brought legal proceedings or made an equivalent claim prior to that date.

This technique would appear first to have been used in this context in Case 4/79 *Providence Agricole de la Champagne v ONIC*,[71]

---

66. [1993] ECR I-4879.
67. [1996] ECR I-2097 at p. 2139.
68. Since Case 40/76 *Kermaschek v Bundesanstalt für Arbeit* [1976] ECR 1669.
69. The basic time limit for a direct action for annulment under Article 173 of the EC Treaty is two months.
70. [1986] ECR 1.
71. [1980] ECR 2823.

where the Court held that the principle underlying Article 174 of the EC Treaty could be invoked by analogy in the context of a declaration of invalidity given on a reference for a preliminary ruling, 'for the same reasons of legal certainty as those which form the basis of that provision'. Under that provision, in the case of a direct action for the annulment of a regulation, the Court may, if it considers it necessary, state which of the effects of the regulation which it has declared void shall be considered as definitive. In *Providence Agricole*, the Court ordered that the invalidity of the Regulation there at issue should only be invoked as from the date of its judgment – with no exceptions in this case for those who had already brought actions.

The problem remains, however, whether the Court may consider on a reference for a preliminary ruling the validity of an act which the parties to the national proceedings *could* have challenged directly. This brings together two different, and potentially conflicting, principles: the principle that the time limits on a direct action for annulment or failure to act should not be circumvented by the use of other remedies by a party who could clearly have brought such an action, which has been accepted with regard to actions for damages, at least in a line of staff cases,[72] and the principle that references for a preliminary ruling are made by the national court, not the parties to the action before the national court.[73] However, the current case-law is stated to be based upon a third principle, that of legal certainty.

This principle was raised in Case C-188/92 *TWD Textilwerke Deggendorf v Bundesminister für Wirtschaft*.[74] There, the Commission had addressed a decision to Germany under the State aids rules of the EC Treaty finding subsidies paid to the applicant to be both procedurally and substantively in breach of the Treaty, and requiring those subsidies to be recovered. A few months later, the German authorities notified the decision to the applicant, and informed it of the possibility of bringing an action for annulment under Article 173, but the applicant did not bring such an action. After a further few months, the relevant German Minister issued a

---

[72.] See e.g. Case 59/65 *Schreckenberg v Commission* [1966] ECR 543, 550; Case 4/67 *Muller (nee Collignon) v Commission* [1967] ECR 365, 373; Case 799/79 *Bruckner v Commission and Council* [1981] ECR 2697; and Case 106/80 *Fournier v Commission* [1981] ECR 2795.

[73.] Case 44/65 *Hessische Knappschaft v Singer* [1965] ECR 965.

[74.] [1994] ECR I-833.

decision effectively requiring the subsidies to be repaid, and the applicant challenged this decision before the German courts, invoking the invalidity of the underlying Commission decision. The question referred to the European Court therefore asked specifically if the validity of the Commission decision could be raised before the national courts.

A.G. Jacobs suggested that to allow a party who could clearly have brought an action for annulment to plead the illegality of such a decision before a national court would enable it to circumvent the fact that the decision had become definitive with regard to that party once the limitation period for an action for annulment had ended. Therefore, for reasons of legal certainty and to preserve the coherence of the Community system of judicial remedies, a party who clearly could have sought the annulment of the decision at issue but failed to do so in time should not be allowed to plead the illegality of that decision before a national court. The European Court followed this approach, holding that here there was no doubt that an action for annulment could have been brought.

A.G. Jacobs suggested that, by limiting this approach to situations where there was no doubt that an action for annulment could be brought, the Court (or the national court) would avoid having to decide whether there was 'direct and individual concern' under Article 173 before allowing a question of invalidity to be raised before it, as feared by some commentators.[75] It may nevertheless be suggested that even to distinguish between cases where there is no doubt and cases where there may be difficulties will require a preliminary investigation of the same sort, particularly since the relevant case-law has not been marked by total consistency.[76] This introduces some of the problems of admissibility which have beset direct actions before the Court and which had previously been remarkably lacking in references for preliminary rulings, and necessarily requires the European Court to go behind the national court's reference to investigate the situation of the parties and the factual background. It may therefore be wondered how far this approach does meet the needs of legal certainty.

---

[75]. See Bebr, 'Direct and indirect control of Community acts in practice' in *The Art of Governance, Festschrift in honour of Eric Stein* (1987) p. 91.

[76]. See Usher, 'Judicial Review of Community Acts and the Private Litigant' in Campbell and Voyatzi (eds) *Legal Reasoning and Judicial Interpretation of European Law – Essays in honour of Lord Mackenzie-Stuart*, (Trenton 1996) pp. 121–48.

CHAPTER FIVE

Procedural rights and privacy

Introduction

This chapter is concerned essentially with those general principles relevant to the conduct of and participation in administrative procedures laid down by Community law. These are principles many of which relate to what might be termed 'natural justice', though that expression has hardly been used by the European Court. In particular, consideration will be given to the right to be heard, arguably the most important right in this area, to the question of legal professional privilege, to rights of privacy, to more general 'rights of the defence' and to the general principle of effective judicial control.

The right to be heard

In an early staff disciplinary case[1] it was stated that, according to a generally accepted principle of administrative law in force in the Member States, the administrations of those States had to allow their servants the opportunity of replying to allegations before any disciplinary decision was taken concerning them, and that this rule, 'which meets the requirements of sound justice and good administration' was to be followed by Community institutions. Rather more surprisingly, it was held that in that case, the failure of the Council to observe this obligation was not sufficient to lead to the annulment of its decision. However, the Court's view of the status and importance of this principle has strengthened over the

---

[1.] Case 32/62 *Alvis* [1963] ECR 49 at p. 55.

years, and by the late 1980s it could say that observance of the right to be heard was, in all proceedings initiated against a person which were liable to culminate in a measure adversely affecting that person, a fundamental principle of Community law which must be guaranteed even in the absence of specific rules.[2]

That broad principle was first established in Case 17/74 *Transocean Marine Paint Association v Commission*,[3] which also shows clearly how it was derived from the national laws of the Member States. In 1967 the Commission had granted an exemption under Article 85(3) of the EC Treaty with regard to the agreement between the undertakings forming the Transocean Marine Paint Association, subject to a condition obliging the Association to keep the Commission informed, *inter alia*, of any change in the composition of its membership.[4] In December 1973[5] this exemption was renewed subject to certain new conditions, including Article 3(1)(d) which required members of the Association to inform the Commission without delay of 'any links by way of common directors or managers between a member of the Association and any other company or firm in the paint sector or any financial participation by a member of the Association in such outside companies or vice versa including all changes in such links or participations already in existence'.

The applicants thought that this raised practical difficulties and could put their exemption at risk, so they brought an action to annul this provision of the decision, on the basis that, since it had neither been mentioned in the Commission's 'Notice of Objections' nor raised at the hearing before the Commission, the Commission had in fact infringed the rules of procedure laid down in Regulation No. 99/63,[6] in particular Articles 2 and 4 thereof. The Commission had in fact indicated that it was willing to renew the exemption for five years, subject to certain fresh conditions and obligations. One of these was that the Association should, according to the literal English translation, 'notify any change in the participatory relationships of the members', which could be interpreted, amongst other things, as requiring merely that the informa-

---

2. See C-85/87 *Dow Benelux v Commission* [1989] ECR 3137 and Case C-142/87 *Belgium v Commission* [1990] ECR I-959.
3. [1974] ECR 1063.
4. Decision of 27 June 1967 (OJ 1967 No. 163, p. 10).
5. Decision of 21 December 1973 (OJ 1974 L19/18).
6. Commission Regulation 99/63 (OJ 1963 p. 2268).

tion which had already had to be supplied under the 1967 decision be supplemented by the notification of any links which might exist between the undertakings which were members of the association.

On the question of Regulation No. 99/63, A.G. Warner suggested in his Opinion,[7] and the Court in fact decided,[8] that Articles 2 and 4 of Regulation No. 99/63 concern the objections which would either bring an agreement within Article 85(1) or prevent it being granted an exemption under Article 85(3) and do not deal with conditions which may be imposed upon a grant of an exemption. However, the Court was not dependent solely upon the arguments which the parties chose to put before it. In this particular case, as A.G. Warner was of the opinion that, at any rate in English law, this would be a situation where *audi alteram partem* could be invoked, he requested the Court's Library and Research Division to make a comparative study of the laws of the other Member States to see whether this was a principle generally accepted in other Member States.

Reference was obviously made in the Opinion to all the well-known English cases on the question.[9] Turning then to the other national legal systems, looking first at French law, it was evident that there were differences of academic opinion. Professor Vedel,[10] was of the opinion that the *audi alteram partem* rule was much wider than the principle of 'droits de la défense' in French law, largely because he was of the view that the doctrine of 'droits de la défense' only applied where the administrative measure in question had been taken by reason of the character or personal conduct of the person concerned. However, other writers took a somewhat wider view, notably Professor Waline, in a contribution to a publication celebrating the centenary of the Luxembourg Conseil d'Etat,[11] where he deduced from the many specific statutory instances, as well as the case-law, that the principle was in the course of development.

In the case of Germany, it may be observed that Article 103 of the Basic Law provided only that the right to be heard applied be-

7. [1974] ECR 1063 at p. 1087.
8. Ibid. at p. 1079.
9. E.g. *Cooper v Wandsworth Board of Works* (1863) 14 CB (NS) 180; *Ridge v Baldwin* [1964] AC 40.
10. *Droit Administratif* (Paris, 1973) p. 281.
11. *Livre Jubilaire* (Luxembourg, 1957) pp. 495–506; see also his *Droit Administratif* (Paris, 9th edition 1969) pp. 460, 552, 586 and 606 for specific examples.

fore the ordinary civil law courts. There was no specific provision for it in administrative law. However, commentators seemed to agree that the principle applied despite the absence of any legislative necessity for it. In fact one textbook[12] managed to quote 14 pre-Federal Republic decisions supporting the general idea that the right to a hearing ('das rechtliche Gehör') was an essential element of correct procedure, not by virtue of principles of written law but by principles of unwritten law, i.e. as a general principle of law.[13]

Similar formulations could be found, for example, in the caselaw of the Luxembourg Council d'Etat, which had held that in the case of administrative decisions which might affect proprietary interests, the administration must hear those affected, even if the actual legislation in question was silent upon the point.[14] The same appeared to be true in Ireland,[15] Scotland[16] and Denmark.[17] As far as Belgian law was concerned, there did not appear to be any decisions directly in point, though academic opinion was in favour of giving a person affected by an administrative decision the right to be heard.[18] In Italy, however, it had been held that the right to be heard was not protected by the Constitution in administrative proceedings[19] and that there was no general principle of administrative law requiring the Administration to communicate preparatory acts to those liable to be affected to enable them to put their view.[20]

Finally, it appeared that no general right to be heard had been developed (perhaps because there were express statutory provisions in many areas) in Dutch administrative law, and this may

---

12. Forsthoff, *Lehrbuch des Verwaltungsrechts* (Munich, 1973) p. 235 *et seq.*

13. See e.g. decision of administrative court of Saxony (Sachs OVG), 24 October 1908 Jahrbuch t. 13 p. 97.

14. 5 August 1966, Aff. No. 5986, *Roth v Ministres de l'Intérieur, de la Santé Publique et des Travaux Publics* – the number of Ministers involved was the result of the subject-matter of the action, a refusal of an authorisation to work a quarry so as to protect underground water supplies.

15. Kelly, *Fundamental Rights in the Irish Law and Constitution* (Dublin, 1961) pp. 313–14.

16. *Malloch v Aberdeen Corporation* [1971] 2 All ER 1278.

17. Andersen, *Dansk Forvaltningsret* (see [1974] ECR 1063 at p. 1088) pp. 377 and 339.

18. See e.g. Dembour, *Droit Administratif* (Liège, 1970) p. 266.

19. Cons. di Stato, Sez. IV, 9 nov. 1971, n. 959, Rass. Cons. di Stato 1971, I, p. 2076.

20. Cons. di Stato, Sez. IV, 15 mai 1970, n. 345, Rass. Cons. di Stato 1970, I, p. 828 (834).

well explain why the Dutch lawyers who appeared for Transocean did not argue that there was a general right to be heard.

A.G. Warner reviewed the position under the various national legal systems in his Opinion and concluded that the right to be heard formed part of those rights which 'the law' referred to in Article 164 of the EC Treaty upholds and of which accordingly it was the duty of the Court to ensure the observance.[21] The way the Court introduced this general principle into its judgment was to state that, notwithstanding the cases specifically dealt with in Articles 2 and 4 of Regulation 99/63, the Regulation was an application of 'the general rule that a person whose interests are perceptibly affected by a decision taken by a public authority must be given the opportunity to make his point of view known'. The Court added that, in the context of an exemption under Article 85(3) of the EC Treaty, this rule required that an undertaking be clearly informed, in good time, of the essence of conditions to which the Commission intended to subject an exemption, and it must have the opportunity to submit its observations to the Commission. The Court took the view that this requirement was not fulfilled, and the condition attached to the exemption was annulled pending reconsideration of the matter by the Commission.

The approach of the Court in this case therefore was to place the express Community legislation in the context of a broader general principle derived from the national laws of the Member States, a clear indication that Community legislation is not to be read in a legal vacuum. However, while the right to be heard has in general been strongly enforced, there is the occasional exception which hardly seems consonant with the principle. In Case 85/76 *Hoffman-la Roche v Commission*,[22] the applicants complained that the Commission had relied on evidence which it had refused to let them inspect on the grounds that it was subject to professional secrecy, with the result that the applicants had not been able to make their views known on the matter. The Court held that the Commission could not rely on such evidence if the refusal of disclosure adversely affected the undertaking's opportunity to make its views known effectively, but then went on to say that 'if such irregularities have in fact been put right during the proceedings before the Court they do not necessarily lead to the annulment of the

---

21. [1974] ECR 1063 at p. 1089.
22. [1979] ECR 461.

contested decision in so far as remedying them at a later stage has not affected the right to be heard'. This hardly seems to accord with the fact that the role of the Court in an action for annulment is to review the legality of the decision at the time it was made, or with the fact that the right to be heard relates to the process leading to the decision at issue, and it is an approach which does not seem to have been followed in more recent case-law.

The general application of the right to be heard in modern case-law is illustrated in Case C-135/92 *Fiskano v Commission*.[23] The action involved a letter sent by the Commission to the Swedish authorities (at a time before Swedish accession), informing them that a particular Swedish fishing boat had been observed fishing in Dutch waters without a licence, and that therefore this boat would not be considered for a new licence for a period of 12 consecutive months. The owners of the boat challenged this decision, arguing, *inter alia*, that they had not been given an opportunity to submit their observations before the decision was adopted. The Court repeated its view that the right to be heard applies in all proceedings initiated against a person which are liable to culminate in a measure adversely affecting that person, and annulled the decision.

In the context of State aids, although it was seen in the previous chapter that the recipient cannot base any legitimate expectations on the unlawful conduct of the national authority which has provided an aid in breach of the Treaty, nevertheless the recipient cannot be required to repay the money unless it has been given the opportunity to state its views. Indeed, Article 93(2) of the EC Treaty expressly requires the Commission to give notice to the parties concerned to submit their comments. If it fails to do so it will breach both the general principle of the right to be heard and the express Treaty provision. In Case C-294/90 *British Aerospace v Commission*,[24] the Commission had issued a decision approving certain aid granted by the British government when Rover Group was acquired by British Aerospace. However, about a year later the Commission discovered that the British government had granted a number of other financial concessions to British Aerospace which had not been notified to it and which, in its view, amounted to an additional £44.4 million of aid. It therefore issued a second decision requiring this aid to be repaid. However, the

Court found that the Commission had not invited British Aerospace to submit its comments as required under Article 93(2), and annulled the decision.

The Council Regulation on dumping[25] similarly gives express rights to be heard and to inspect certain information, but in Case C-49/88 *Al-Jubail v Council*[26] it was stated that in interpreting the provision in the Regulation, it was necessary 'to take account in particular of the requirements stemming from the right to a fair hearing, a principle whose fundamental character has been stressed on numerous occasions in the case-law of the Court'. The Court added that, with regard to the right to a fair hearing, the Community institutions had to be all the more scrupulous in view of the fact that the rules as they stood at that time[27] did not provide all the guarantees for the protection for the individual which might exist in certain national systems. On the facts of the case, the Court concluded that there was nothing to show that the Community institutions had discharged their duty to place at the applicants' disposal all the information which would have enabled them effectively to defend their interests, and annulled the provision imposing an anti-dumping duty on them.

However, in the formulation used by the Court, only those adversely affected by a measure benefit from the right to a fair hearing. In the context of anti-dumping measures, the Court of First Instance[28] rejected an independent importer's plea of a breach of its right to a fair hearing as unfounded, in that anti-dumping proceedings and any protective measures adopted at the end of such proceedings are directed only against foreign producers and exporters or such from non-Member countries as well as, where relevant, associated importers, and not against independent importers such as the applicant. The anti-dumping proceeding was not against the applicant and could not therefore result in a measure adversely affecting it, since no allegation was made against it.

However, the current formulation of the Regulation gives rights to 'interested parties' to make their views known in writing and to receive the text of the complaint[29] and gives the complainants, importers and exporters and their representative associations, users

25. See Article 6 of Council Regulation 3283/94 on dumping (OJ 1994 L349/1).
26. [1991] ECR I-3187 at p. 3241.
27. Article 7(4)(a) and (b) of Council Regulation 2176/84.
28. Case T-167/94 *Nölle v Council and Commission* [1995] ECR II-2615.
29. Council Regulation 3283/94, Article 5(10) and (11).

and consumer organisations which have made themselves known, the right to inspect and respond to information made available by the parties.[30] On the other hand, a right to a hearing in a literal sense is given only to interested parties who have made a written request for a hearing showing that they are likely to be affected by the result of the proceedings and that there are particular reasons why they should be heard.

It may therefore be concluded that express procedural rules with regard the right to submit observations or receive information should be read in the light of the general principle of the right to a fair hearing, but that the express rules may sometimes go further than the general principle.

Other rights of the defence

While, as will have been seen from the *Transocean* case, the French concept of 'droits de la défense' may overlap with aspects of the right to be heard, it does also extend to other procedural rights for which the literal English translation 'rights of defence' has been used in the English versions. In Case C-374/87 *Orkem v Commission*,[31] the Court recognised that it was necessary not only to protect rights of defence in administrative procedures which might lead to the imposition of penalties, but also to prevent those rights being irremediably impaired during preliminary inquiry procedures. In that context, it has effectively accepted a limited privilege against self-incrimination. It there held in the context of competition proceedings that while the Commission was entitled to compel an undertaking to provide all necessary information, even if that information might be used to establish the existence of anti-competitive conduct, it could not, by means of a request for information, undermine the rights of defence of the undertaking concerned and compel it to provide answers which might involve an admission on its part of the existence of an infringement which it was incumbent on the Commission to prove. In the light of this, questions for example asking when meetings were held and in what capacity the participants attended were regarded as intended only to secure factual information, but questions asking about the

---

30. Ibid. Article 6(7).
31. [1989] ECR 3283, paras 34 and 35.

adoption of concerted measures or about the attribution of targets or quotas to the participants were regarded as being intended to compel the applicant to acknowledge its participation in an illegal agreement and as therefore undermining the applicant's right of defence.

Legal professional privilege

The concept of legal professional privilege accepted as a general principle of Community is also categorised by the European Court as an aspect of the right of defence, and shows very clearly that general principles as adapted into EC law may not be identical to the national principles on which they are based. In Case 155/79 *AM & S Europe v Commission*[32] the European Court defined the scope of legal professional privilege in EC law, and also confirmed the procedure by which a claim of such privilege may be protected. In brief, following an on-the-spot investigation under Regulation 17/62, the Commission requested AM&S to produce certain documents, and ultimately issued a formal Decision to that effect under Article 14(3) of Regulation 17/62,[33] whilst AM&S claimed that the documents were 'covered by the doctrine of legal privilege' and, after refusing to produce them, sought the annulment of the provision in the Commission's Decision requiring their production. The documents concerned fell into four main categories: solicitors' instructions to counsel; communications between an outside solicitor and AM&S or one of its parent companies containing legal advice or requests for legal advice; documents containing legal advice or requests for legal advice from or to an 'in-house' lawyer employed by AM&S or one of its parent companies; and communications between executives of AM&S or one of its parent companies recording legal advice or requests for legal advice.

In effect, AM&S and the Commission were originally in dispute not so much as to the existence of a principle of legal professional privilege but rather as to the procedure whereby it should be determined whether or not a document was protected from disclosure, and it was the French government, intervening to support the Commission, which raised the fundamental issue of principle. Fol-

---

[32]. [1982] ECR 1575.
[33]. OJ 204/62.

lowing an interim order in which it required the documents to be produced to it in sealed envelopes,[34] it was the issue of principle which the European Court dealt with at greatest length in its final judgment. It was expressly stated that Community law derives not only from the economic but also the legal 'interpenetration' of the Member States; hence, in this case, account had to be taken of the principles and concepts common to the laws of the Member States concerning the observance of confidentiality as regards communications between lawyer and client. It should be noted, however, that the Court took from the outset the view that the purpose of the protection of confidentiality is to enable any person, without constraint, 'to consult a lawyer whose profession entails the giving of *independent* legal advice to all those in need of it' (emphasis added). After noting that in some States, protection against disclosure is regarded as being derived from the very nature of the legal profession, whereas in others it is based upon 'the rights of the defence' (i.e. the protection of individual litigants, in particular their right to be heard) the Court concluded that what was common to the laws of the Member states was the protection of written communications between lawyer and client subject to two conditions: the communications must be made 'for the purpose and in the interest of the client's rights of defence' and 'they must emanate from independent lawyers, that is to say, lawyers who are not bound to the client by a relationship of employment'.

In the context of competition proceedings before the Commission, the Court was willing to accept that the principle of 'confidentiality' must be recognised as covering all written communications exchanged after the initiation of the administrative procedure under Regulation No. 17 which may lead to a decision on the application of Articles 85 and 86, which presumably means from notification or application from receipt of a complaint or from the commencement of proceedings on the Commission's own initiative;[35] the Court also accepted that it could apply to earlier written communications relating to the subject matter of such a procedure, and in this case it was found that the documents in question – which were apparently drawn up during the period immediately before and after the Accession of the United Kingdom to the Community and were principally concerned with avoiding con-

---

34. [1982] ECR at p. 1616 (order of 4 February 1981).
35. See Articles 2, 3 and 4 of Regulation 17.

flicts between the applicant and the Community authorities with regard to the competition rules – were sufficiently connected with the procedure to be protected from disclosure. Though perhaps not wholly relevant, this protection of pre-dispute advice contrasts somewhat with the Court's views on costs, since it has long held that remuneration for legal advice given before the commencement of litigation is not recoverable.[36]

The second condition itself gives rise to two problems, the definition of a lawyer, and the question of his or her independence. The emphasis on independence, quite simply defined as not being bound to the client by a relationship of employment, appears to reflect the Court's view of the purpose of legal professional privilege, as has been noted, and may not be unconnected with the fact that in some Member States, lawyers may not enter into contracts of employment, although a salaried solicitor in an independent firm of solicitors would appear to be protected. More particularly, the Court states that the requirement of independence 'is based on a conception of the lawyer's role as collaborating in the administration of justice by the courts, and as being required to provide, in full independence, and in the overriding interests of that case, such legal assistance as the client needs'. This might almost seem to treat confidentiality as a protection of the independence of the lawyer, but such a view hardly squares with the fact that later in the judgment it was held to be open to the client to waive the privilege. Be that as it may, the practical consequences for many large undertakings employing 'in-house' lawyer is that their advice will not be protected.

With regard to the definition of a 'lawyer', the Court stated that the protection of written communications between lawyer and client must apply to 'any lawyer entitled to practise his profession in one of the Member States, regardless of the Member State in which the client lives'. Although the phrase 'practise his profession' could be open to a wide interpretation and although English is the language of the case, it should be noted that the French version of the judgment refers to an 'avocat inscrit au barreau' of a Member State, the phrase used in Article 17 of the EC Statute of the Court, and the parallel provisions of the other Statutes, and there rendered into English as 'a lawyer entitled to practise before a Court of a Member State'. Moreover, the Court emphasised that

---

[36.] See Case 75/69 *Hake v Commission* [1970] ECR 901 at pp. 902–3.

the protection of confidentiality had as its counterpart 'the rules of professional ethics and discipline which are laid down and enforced in the general interest by the institutions endowed with the requisite powers for that purpose' and referred expressly to Article 17 of the Statute as demonstrating this conception. It may also be noted that the Court cited Council Directive 77/249/EC[37] on the provision of services by lawyers as determining the limits beyond which the protection of confidentiality may not be extended. The result of all this appears to be that, for his communication to be protected, the independent lawyer must be qualified, and entitled to practise on of the professions listed in Directive 77/249, in a Member State, he must be subject to the professional discipline of that profession, and he must be acting within the scope of the Directive. Hence communications from an American lawyer, for example, not qualified in a Member State, would not be protected; more contentiously, it may be doubted whether communications from a lawyer qualified in one Member State, but practising in another Member State not under the terms of the services Directive but by pursuing activities to which access is not restricted,[38] would be protected.

Finally, the influence of the 'rights of the defence' may be seen in the fact, already alluded to, that in the view of the Court, the protection exists for the benefit of the client rather than the lawyer, despite the emphasis on the lawyer's independence. It was stated that 'the principle of confidentiality does not prevent a lawyer's client from disclosing the written communications between them if he considers that it is in his interests to do so', which is exactly the same view as the Court has taken with regard to the confidentiality of medical information, which has been held to exist for the benefit of the patient, not the doctor.[39]

Privacy

The question of privacy has also arisen in the context of inspections under the competition rules, in Cases 46/87 and 227/88

---

37. OJ 1977 L78/17.
38. See Usher, 'Establishment, Services and Lawyers' (1979) *Scots Law Times* 65 at pp. 69–70.
39. See Case 155/78 *M v Commission* [1980] ECR 1797.

Hoechst v Commission.[40] There the applicant claimed, *inter alia*, that the search of its premises was a breach of the fundamental right to the inviolability of the home, and more particularly an infringement of Article 8 of the European Convention on Human Rights, declaring that 'everyone has the right to respect for his private and family life, his home and his correspondence'.

After repeating its previous case-law, the Court dealt with these points very briefly. It suggested that while the inviolability of the home must be recognised in the Community legal order as a principle common to the laws of the Member States 'in regard to the private dwellings of natural persons', the same was not true with regard to undertakings, given that there were divergences between the legal systems of the Member States with regard to the nature and degree of protection afforded to business premises against intervention by the public authorities. The Court similarly held Article 8(1) of the Human Rights Convention to be concerned with the development of man's personal freedom, and it could not therefore be extended to business premises, adding that there was no case-law of the European Court of Human Rights on the matter. It has been pointed out that this last statement was factually inaccurate,[41] since the Court of Human Rights had given judgment in the *Chappell* case[42] a few months earlier, which concerned the application of Article 8 to the seizure of video-cassettes and documents from premises part of which were used as offices. It is perhaps of significance that the matter was considered under Article 8, even if the Human Rights Court did not discuss as such the question whether commercial premises fell within its ambit. On the other hand, to put the matter in context, A.G. Mischo did carry out a detailed analysis of rights of entry into business premises in the Member States,[43] concluding, as the Commission was prepared to concede, that while there was a fundamental right to the inviolability of business premises, it did not apply to the same extent as to a private dwelling, and that in the economic, fiscal and social spheres there were many measures providing for inspections of various types. He eventually suggested that the rights of undertakings were sufficiently protected by the possibility af-

---

40. [1989] ECR 2859.
41. Clapham, *Human Rights and the European Community: A Critical Overview* (Baden-Baden, 1991) p. 59.
42. Judgment of 30 March 1989, Series A, Vol. 152.
43. [1989] ECR at pp. 2884–94.

forded to them of contesting before the Court (now the Court of First Instance) the validity of decisions ordering investigations and applying for suspension of their operation.

However, whatever the situation under the Convention, the Court did recognise that all the legal systems of the Member States provided for protection against arbitrary or disproportionate intervention in the sphere of private activities of any person, and that the need for such protection must be recognised as a general principle of Community law; it further pointed out that it had already held under the Coal and Steel Treaty that it had power to determine whether measures of investigation taken by the Commission were excessive.[44] It is, nevertheless, perhaps slightly surprising that while in general the Court has insisted that it is the principles underlying rules of national or international law which must be observed in the context of Community law rather than national or international rules as such, that it was held that if the Commission is carrying out an investigation with the assistance of the national authorities under Article 14(6) of Regulation 17/62 against the wishes of the undertaking concerned, it must respect the relevant procedural guarantees laid down by the relevant national law.

Effective judicial protection

The overarching procedural guarantee is the principle of effective judicial protection. However, while the procedural rights described above have been essentially concerned with the conduct by Community institutions of procedures laid down by Community law, the principle of effective judicial protection has also been used in the context of Member States acting within the scope of Community law.

An illustration involving the United Kingdom may be found in the judgment of the Court concerning Mrs. Johnston's attempts to continue as a policewoman in Northern Ireland.[45] Mrs. Johnston was faced with a certificate issued by the Secretary of State under the Northern Ireland Sex Discrimination Order stating that this certificate was 'conclusive evidence' that the conditions for derogating from the principle of equal treatment were fulfilled. In that

---

44. Cases 5–11 and 13–15/62 *San Michele v Commission* [1962] ECR 449.
45. Case 222/84 *Johnston v Chief Constable of the RUC* [1986] ECR 1651.

context, the Court held that a provision of an EC Directive, which required Member States to enable all persons who consider themselves wronged by sex discrimination to be able to pursue their claims by judicial process, was a reflection of a general principle of law underlying the constitutional traditions common to the Member States, and underlying also specific provisions of the Human Rights Convention. The Court concluded that this general principle of effective judicial control meant that a certificate which claimed to be conclusive could not allow the competent authority to deprive an individual of the possibility of asserting by judicial process the rights conferred by the directive. The necessary implication is that the tradition in the United Kingdom that an administrative authority may issue a supposedly conclusive certificate does not accord with this general principle of effective judicial control.

However, the principle does not just apply at the national level. It goes to the heart of the European Court's own jurisdiction and it may be suggested that the principle underlies the Court's assumption of jurisdiction over acts of the European Parliament in Case 294/83 *Les Verts v European Parliament*,[46] where the Court took as its starting point the premise that the Community is based on the rule of law, in that 'neither its Member States nor its institutions can avoid a review of the question whether the measures adopted by them are in conformity with the basic constitutional charter, the Treaty'. The case involved a challenge by the French Greens to decisions of, and rules adopted by, the European Parliament concerning appropriations granted as a contribution to the information campaign for the second direct elections to the Parliament. Despite the silence of Article 173 of the then EEC Treaty, which referred only to acts of the Council and the Commission, the Court held that the general scheme of the Treaty was to make a direct action available against all measures adopted by the institutions which were intended to have legal effects. The Court suggested that the European Parliament was not expressly mentioned amongst the institutions whose measures might be contested because in its original version the EEC Treaty merely granted it powers of consultation and political control, rather than the power to adopt measures intended to have legal effects vis-à-vis third parties.

Since, unlike the Coal and Steel Treaty, the EEC Treaty con-

---

46. [1986] ECR 1339.

tained only one provision relating to an action for annulment, Article 173, the Court held that this provision must be regarded as being of general application. It further held that an interpretation of it which excluded measures adopted by the European Parliament from those which could be contested would lead to a result contrary both to the spirit of the Treaty and to its system. If Article 173 were not so extended, measures adopted by the European Parliament in the context of the EEC Treaty could trespass into the powers of the Member States or of the other institutions or exceed the limits set for the Parliament's powers, without it being possible to refer them for review by the Court.

The Court went on to conclude that an action for annulment must lie against measures adopted by the European Parliament intended to have legal effects with regard to third parties. With regard to the particular decisions and rules of the European Parliament at issue, the Court held that they governed the rights and obligations both of those political groupings that were already represented in the European Parliament, and of those which wished to take part in the 1984 direct elections. The measures were therefore designed to produce legal effects with regard to third parties and could be the subject of an action for annulment under Article 173. In other words, so as to ensure a comprehensive system of judicial control of acts of the Community institutions affecting the legal situation of third parties, the European Court rewrote Article 173 so as to include the European Parliament as the author of a challengeable act. A formal rewriting followed in the Treaty amendments agreed at Maastricht in 1991, so that under what is now Article 173 of the EC Treaty the Court may review the legality of 'acts of the European Parliament intended to produce legal effects vis-à-vis third parties' – a term which precisely reflects its judgment.

CHAPTER SIX

Property rights

Treaty provisions

It is stated in Article 222 of the EC Treaty that 'this Treaty shall in no way prejudice the rules in Member States governing the system of property ownership'.

However, it soon became evident that there was potential for conflict between the prohibition of measures equivalent to quantitative restrictions in trade between Member States set out in Articles 30 to 36 of the EC Treaty, and restrictions on import or export between Member States imposed by traders pursuant to intellectual or industrial property rights. The approach of the Court from its earliest decision on industrial property rights in Case 78/70 *Deutsche Grammophon v Metro-SB-Grossmarkte*,[1] was to hold that it was not the *existence* of industrial property rights which might conflict with the Treaty, but their *exercise*. In the light of this distinction, the Court developed the view that what should be protected was the 'specific subject-matter' of the right, which it defined as the right of the holder of a trademark, or patent, or similar right, to put the goods protected by the patent or trademark into circulation for the first time. However, once the good had been marketed in the Community by the owner of the patent or trademark or with his consent, the owner could not use parallel patents or trademarks in other Member States to prevent the goods being re-sold there.[2] In other words, from the early 1970s, holders of industrial and intellectual property rights have in effect been required to treat the Community as a single market.

[1.] [1971] ECR 487.
[2.] Case 15/74 *Centrafarm v Sterling Drug* [1974] ECR 1147.

There is a certain parallelism between this interpretation of the Treaty provisions and the development of a general principle of the protection of property rights in Community law, in that while property rights are in principle to be respected, it has been accepted that limits may be placed on the exercise of those rights in the broader Community interest.

Development of the general principle

The essentials of the recognition of property rights as a general principle of Community law are to be found in Case 44/79 *Hauer v Land Rheinland-Pfalz*,[3] even though the matter was not directly raised in the two questions referred to the European Court by the Verwaltungsgericht of Neustadt an der Weinstrasse. The background was that Mrs. Hauer, in 1975, applied to the Land authorities for permission to start growing vines on her property in Bad Durkheim, such permission having a few days earlier been granted to the owners of some neighbouring land. Under the relevant German legislation, vines could only be cultivated on land recognised as being suitable therefor, and the Land authorities turned down her application in January 1976 on the ground that her property was not suitable. Mrs. Hauer put in a formal complaint objecting to the decision in her case, later that same month, and her complaint was rejected in October 1976, this time not only on the ground that her land was not suitable, but also on the ground that Council Regulation 1162/76 on measures designed to adjust vine-growing potential to market requirements,[4] which had been enacted in the meantime, prohibited all new planting of vine varieties classed as wine grape varieties, and also prohibited the grant of authorisation for such new plantings.

Mrs. Hauer thereupon commenced proceedings before her local administrative court. During the course of the proceedings, the Land indicated that it would after all be willing to grant the necessary authorisation under the German legislation once the prohibition on planting new vines under Regulation 1162/76 had elapsed; it might, however, be noted that by the time the European Court delivered its judgment, the period of that prohibition had been extended until the end of December 1979.

3. [1979] ECR 3727.
4. OJ 1976 L 135/32.

Hence, the remaining obstacle facing Mrs. Hauer was the Regulation, and it was argued on her behalf that it did not apply to her situation, since her application had been lodged before its entry into force, and that in any event it was incompatible with various provisions of the German Basic Law. The specific questions referred to the European Court by the Verwaltungsgericht related, however, to the interpretation of the Regulation rather than to its validity. The first asked, reflecting Mrs. Hauer's argument, whether the prohibition on new plantings of vines applied where permission to grow vines had been requested before the entry into force of the Regulation, and the second asked whether it applied generally, i.e. irrespective of whether the land in question was regarded as suitable for cultivating vines, within the meaning of the German legislation.

The Court was able to deal relatively briefly with these two questions, finding that the prohibitions in the Regulation did indeed apply where permission to plant vines had been sought before its entry into force, and that they applied irrespective of the nature of the land in question. This, however, brought the Court to the real crux of the matter. In its order for reference, the Verwaltungsgericht had indicated that if the Regulation was so interpreted, it might not be applicable in Germany on the grounds that it was not compatible with Articles 12 and 14 of the German Basic Law, concerning rights of property and the right to carry on a business activity. Hence the Court found itself faced once again with the problem of the relationship between Community law and principles of the German Basic law which had been encountered in particular in the *Internationale Handelsgesellschaft* [5] and *Nold* [6] cases. In resolving it, the differing formulations, negative in the former and positive in the latter, which had been used in the two cases were repeated and brought together.

Paraphrasing its judgment in *Internationale Handelsgesellschaft*, the Court said that the question whether fundamental rights had been breached by a Community act could only be determined within the framework of Community law itself, and that to have recourse to criteria from the legislation or constitutional system of one particular Member State would have an adverse effect on the uniformity and efficiency of Community law. On the other hand,

5. [1970] ECR 1125. See Chapter 3 above.
6. [1974] ECR 491.

it refrained from repeating expressly that 'the validity of a Community measure ... cannot be affected by allegations that it runs counter to ... fundamental rights as formulated by the constitution of [a Member] State',[7] although the terms used were still negative. It could be suggested that this approach has unnecessarily given rise to the impression that fundamental rights in national law are not taken into account in assessing the validity of Community rules, whereas the true position can be stated in positive terms as being that fundamental principles of national law *are* taken into account as sources of general principles of Community law, but that the European Court has no power to apply them as rules of national law.[8] Indeed, as has been observed, what actually happened in *Internationale Handelsgesellschaft* was that the European Court applied the principle of proportionality, the fundamental principle at issue, but as a rule of Community law rather than of German law.

A more positive approach had in fact been used in *Nold*, and the Court quoted passages from its judgment in that case verbatim, repeating that fundamental rights form an integral part of the general principles of law of which it ensures the observance, and that in safeguarding these rights it is bound to draw inspiration from constitutional traditions common to the Member States, and that it cannot uphold measures which are incompatible with fundamental rights recognised and protected by the constitutions of these States. It also repeated that 'international treaties for the protection of human rights on which the Member States have collaborated or of which they are signatories, can supply guidelines which should be followed within the framework of Community Law',[9] and noted that this approach had been approved in the Joint Declaration on fundamental rights made by the European Parliament, the Council and the Commission on 5 April 1977,[10] which referred expressly to the European Convention on Human Rights. This is now, of course, overtaken by the express terms of the Maastricht Treaty.

The Court in fact took the Verwaltungsgericht's doubts as to the compatibility of the Regulation with provisions of the German Basic Law as an invitation for it to assess its validity in terms of

---

7. [1970] ECR 1125 at p. 1134.
8. Usher 'The Influence of National Concepts on Decisions of the European Court' (1976) EL Rev 359 at p. 373.
9. [1974] ECR 491 at p. 507.
10. OJ 1977 C103/1.

principles of Community Law. So doing, it turned first to the question of rights of property in the Community system, taking as its starting point Article 1 of the First Protocol to the Human Rights Convention, which it described as reflecting the concepts common to the constitutions of the Member States.[11] It noted that while this provision recognised that 'every natural or legal person is entitled to the peaceful enjoyment of his possessions', it nonetheless preserved the 'right of a State to enforce such laws as it deems necessary to control the use of property in accordance with the general interest'. Nonetheless, although it took the view that the Regulation amounted to a control on use of property, the Court felt that the rule in the Convention did not enable it to give a sufficiently precise answer to the problem and so it considered also the rules applied in the various Member states. This it did not merely in general terms, but by reference to specific provisions of, in this case, the German, Italian and Irish constitutions, which would appear to represent a reversion to a practice hardly encountered since the early days of the ECSC Treaty.[12] A possible explanation of this more open approach by the Court itself may be that it represented an attempt to reassure those national courts which feared that their fundamental principles were threatened by the primacy of Community law that in practice these principles were taken into account at the Community level. The conclusion the Court drew from its analysis was that property ownership is subject to inherent obligations, to social requirements, and the requirements of the common good. It further noted that all the wine-producing countries of the Community imposed restrictions on the planting of vines, selection of varieties and methods of cultivation, and that nowhere were these restrictions regarded as necessarily infringing property rights.

On the basis that Regulation 1162/76 was an example of this type of restriction, the Court then considered whether the prohibitions introduced were appropriate to the aims pursued by the Community viticultural legislation which were to establish a lasting balance in the wine market, and to improve the quality of wine

---

11. In Case 36/75 *Rutili* [1975] ECR 1219 the Court had described the Community rules limiting the powers of Member States with regard to the movements of migrant workers as being specific manifestation of the principle embodied in Articles 8 to 11 of the Convention.
12. See Joined Cases 7/56 and 3-75/57 *Algera v Assembly* [1957 and 1958] ECR 39 at pp. 55–6.

put on the market. In this context, Regulation 1162/76 was a temporary measure aimed at preventing any increase in the overproduction which already existed. It was thus held not to be an undue restriction on the exercise of property rights, being justified by the aims the Community was pursuing in the general interest. In this, the Court agreed both with the Opinion of A.G. Capotorti and indeed with the observations put in by the German government.

The Court then turned to the question whether the Regulation constituted a breach of the right to the free pursuit of business activity. This was the selfsame principle that had been at issue in *Nold*, and the Court repeated its statement in that decision that far from constituting an unfettered prerogative, such a right 'must be viewed in the light of the social function of the ... activities protected thereunder'.[13] In this context, it was pointed out that the Regulation did not prevent anyone from cultivating existing vineyards, and in so far as the prohibition on new planting affected the freedom to carry on the activity of viticulture it was the natural consequence of the limitations on property rights, and was justified for the same reasons.

Thus, in the Community, as in the Member States, rights of property and the freedom to carry out business activities, may be subjected to restrictive measures taken by the relevant authorities in the general interest, although it appears that in the Community context it must be shown that such restrictive measures are not only in the general interest, but also comply with the aims of Community policy and are not out of proportion to the end they seek to achieve; in more English terminology, they must not be unreasonable.

A.G. Capotorti did discuss whether compensation should have been payable for such a limitation of property rights, but concluded that this would only be the case where the measure amounted to expropriation, which he did not consider to be the situation here.[14]

This approach has been subsequently maintained. In Case C-265/87 *Schrader*,[15] where the Court repeated that both the right to property and the freedom to pursue a trade or profession form part of the general principles of Community law. However, it

---

[13] [1974] ECR 491 at 508.
[14] [1979] ECR at p. 3762.
[15] [1989] ECR 2237.

pointed out that those principles do not constitute an unfettered prerogative, but must be viewed in the light of the social function of the activities protected thereunder. Consequently, the right to property and the freedom to pursue a trade or profession may be restricted, particularly in the context of a common organisation of the market, 'provided that those restrictions in fact correspond to objectives of general interest pursued by the Community and that they do not constitute a disproportionate and intolerable interference which infringes upon the very substance of the rights guaranteed'. It may be suggested that the concept of the 'very substance' of a property right corresponds to the 'specific subject-matter' of a property right developed in the intellectual property case-law discussed in the first part of this chapter.

Limits on the substance of property rights were indicated in Case C-280/93 *Germany v Council*,[16] where Germany argued that the introduction of the common organisation of the market in bananas deprived traders who traditionally marketed third country bananas of their market shares and therefore breached their property rights. The Court, however, asserted that no economic operator could claim a right to property in a market share which he held at a time before the establishment of a common organisation of a market, since such a market share constituted only a momentary economic position exposed to the risks of changing circumstances.

Perhaps the most extreme limit on the exercise of property rights in Community law involved the impounding of an aircraft in Case C-84/95 *Bosphorus Hava Yollari Turiszm ve Ticaret AS v Minister for Transport, Energy and Communications, Ireland and the Attorney General*.[17] Acting under Council Regulation 990/93, which gave effect to a number of UN Security Council regulations, imposing a trade and financial embargo on the Federal Republic of Yugoslavia (Serbia and Montenegro), the Irish Government decided to impound at Dublin airport an aircraft operated by the Turkish airline Bosphorus on the ground that since it was leased from Yugoslav Airlines (JAT), it was therefore an aircraft in which a majority or controlling interest was held by a person or undertaking in or operating from the Federal Republic of Yugoslavia. It was accepted that Bosphorus was an entirely innocent party and

16. [1994] ECR I-4973.
17. [1996] ECR I-3953.

was not in any way seeking to break UN sanctions. Bosphorus challenged the decision before an Irish court, which referred the matter to the Court.

Bosphorus invoked in particular to the right to peaceful enjoyment of property and the right to pursue a commercial activity. Referring to the text of Article 1 of the First Protocol to the Convention and the relevant case law of the European Court of Human Rights, A.G. Jacobs concluded that the right to peaceful enjoyment of possessions covered the type of interest which Bosphorus had in the impounded aircraft. However, he noted that the European Court of Human Rights had also recognised that an appropriate balance had to be struck between the demands of the general interest of the community and the requirements of the protection of the individual's fundamental rights. After reviewing a number of decisions of the Court of Human Rights and the Court of Justice in which that issue had arisen, A.G. Jacobs concluded that the essential question was whether the interference with Bosphorus Airways' possession of the aircraft was a proportionate measure in the light of the aims of general interest which the Regulation sought to achieve. Thus the principle of proportionality, plead by Bosphorus as a separate head, was in fact an essential part of the test to be applied in reviewing the legitimacy of the limits placed on the exercise of its property rights, and this was the approach followed also by the European Court in its judgment.

Undertaking a balancing of interests, both A.G. Jacobs and the Court noted the particularly strong public interest in enforcing embargo measures to put an end to the state of war in the region, and observed that any measure imposing sanctions has, by definition, consequences which affect the right to property thereby causing harm to persons in no way responsible for the situation. In the light of the fundamental general interest at issue, it was concluded that the impounding of the aircraft in question could not be regarded as inappropriate or disproportionate.

Community quotas and property rights

It has been observed that 'it is impossible to ignore the vigorous trade in quota which has developed in some Member States',[18]

18. Cardwell, *Milk Quotas* (Oxford, 1996) p. 91.

which may be contrasted with the view of the Court of Auditors that this trade in quotas prevented the system being fully effective to reduce over-production.[19] While it is not appropriate here to enter into a detailed discussion of the common organisation of the market in milk and milk products, what is of interest in the context of general principles of Community law is the extent to which a measure intended to reduce production may be regarded, as a matter of Community law, as giving rise to property rights which should be protected.

The system of milk quotas is entirely a creature of European Community Law. It was introduced by EEC Council legislation in 1984,[20] which, with the aim of reducing the excessive output of milk and milk products, provided for the imposition of a punitive levy on producers or purchasers exceeding defined reference quantities, with the proviso that the levy on the purchaser was to be passed on to the producer. The question of property rights arose from the fact that the existence of milk-quota depends upon a combination of a producer and a holding.

The initial allocation of quota in April 1984 depended on deliveries or direct sales by the producer during the relevant reference year. However, while the initial allocation depended on the activities of the producer, subsequent transfer was defined in the Community legislation in terms of the holding. Article 7, paragraph 1 of Council Regulation 857/84 provided that where a holding was sold, leased or transferred by inheritance, all or part of the corresponding reference quantity should be transferred to the purchaser, tenant or heir according to procedures to be determined. There were a limited number of exceptions, but it may be observed that the Council Regulations themselves were silent about reversion to the landlord at the expiry of a lease, and about compensation for a departing tenant who did not intend to continue milk production. However, the Commission implementing Regulation 1371/84 referred in its Article 5(3) to other cases of transfer which had 'comparable legal effects' so far as producers were concerned.

The questions of reversion, compensation and property rights arose in Case 5/88 *Wachauf v Bundesamt für Ernährung und Fort-*

[19.] Court of Auditors, Special Report 4/93 on the implementation of the quota system intended to control milk production (OJ 1994 C12/1).

[20.] Council Regulation 857/84, now repealed and replaced by Council Regulation 3950/92, as amended.

wirtschaft.[21] In its judgment in that case, the European Court expressly accepted that the reversion of a holding at the expiry of a lease did give rise to 'comparable legal effects' to the types of transfer listed in the Regulation, so that in principle the quota would go with the holding. It further held that, at least where the allocation of the quota was the result of the tenant's own labours, it would be a breach of the tenant's fundamental rights to deprive him of the fruits of his labour without compensation. However, the Court concluded that the Community legislation in fact left the Member States enough discretion to ensure that the tenant was able either to keep all or part of his quota or to receive compensation if he gave it up. It should be observed that the Court also held, presumably because the dispute arose in the context of a national outgoers' scheme, that the part of the quota for which the tenant received compensation could not be transferred to the landlord, but should be treated as being released. The United Kingdom scheme introduced by the Agriculture Act 1986 does provide a mechanism by which a tenant receives compensation for some of the quota, but it provides for the compensation to be paid by the landlord, to whom the quota is then transferred.

It has subsequently become clear that the Court's use of the phrase 'fruits of his labour' in *Wachauf* is both precise and important. The Court was not recognising that quota as such was a property right but that in that particular case, where the holding had not been let as a dairy unit, and it was the tenant who had acquired and introduced the dairy cows and the technical facilities required for milk production, the quota represented the fruits of the tenant's labour.

This follows from the decision in Case C-2/92 *R v MAFF, ex p Bostock*,[22] which involved the termination of a lease of a holding which had been let as a dairy farm in England before the Agriculture Act 1986 entered into force. The quota therefore reverted with the holding to the landlord with no express provision as to compensation, and the tenant argued that this was a breach of the general principle of respect for property in Community law. While the Court did reaffirm that the requirements flowing from the protection of fundamental rights in the Community legal order are also binding on Member States when they implement Community

---

[21.] [1989] ECR 2609.
[22.] [1994] ECR I-35.

rules, it did not accept the tenant's argument that protection of the right of property required the Member State to make provision for compensation to be paid to the outgoing tenant by the landlord or to confer on the tenant a direct right to claim compensation from the landlord. After emphasising that *Wachauf* was concerned with the protection of the fruits of the tenant's labours, the Court held that the right to property safeguarded by the Community legal order does not include the right to dispose, for profit, of an advantage such as reference quantities allocated in the context of the common organisation of a market, which does not derive from the assets or occupational activity of the person concerned.[23]

A similar view was taken with regard to the introduction of a system of premium rights (production quotas) attributed to the producers of sheepmeat, goatmeat or beef and veal in Case C-38/94 *R v Minister for Agriculture, Fisheries and Food, ex p Country Landowner's Association*.[24] Here the premium rights could be transferred by the producer with the holding or, subject to surrendering a proportion of the rights transferred to the national reserve, without transferring the holding. The landowners claimed that Member States should be required to introduce a compensation mechanism for the loss suffered by the owners of agricultural land in particular where the premium right was transferred by producers who did not own the land on which they farmed. The landowners argued that the allocation of freely transferable quotas to tenant producers would have the effect of reducing the capital value of the land. This point was accepted by the Ministry of Agriculture, Fisheries and Food but they refuted the existence of any obligation upon them to compensate the landowners for this loss. The Court reaffirmed its jurisprudence in the *Bostock* case, declaring that no general principle of law upheld by the Community legal order, in particular, the principle of protection of the right to property, required that such compensation be paid. On the other hand, it stated that it was for each Member State to assess the need for such measures having regard in particular to the national arrangements for implementing the rules in question and the national rules governing the relationship between landlord and tenant.

---

23. See also Case C-44/89 *Von Deetzen v Hauptzollamt Hamburg-Jonas (Von Deetzen II)* [1991] ECR I-5119 at para. 27.
24. [1995] ECR I-3875.

Finally, in Case C-63/93 *Duff and others v Minister for Agriculture and Food, Ireland and The Attorney General*[25] where it was alleged, *inter alia*, that the failure to grant additional milk-quota to producers who had adopted development plans under Community law infringed their property rights, the Court held that the rules in question did not affect the *substance* of the right to property as the rules were aimed at the general Community interest and allowed the producers to continue to produce milk at the level of their production prior to the entry into force of the new rules (paragraph 30).

The overall conclusion therefore is that although Community institutions and Member States acting within the scope of Community law are required to respect property rights, the exercise of those rights may be subjected to considerable restrictions if they are justified in the general interest.

25. [1996] ECR I-569.

CHAPTER SEVEN

Principles of good administration

Introduction

The aim of this chapter is to examine the extent to which Community law has developed a general theory of good administration, a term frequently found in judgments of the European Court, and often used in conjunction with the general principles discussed in the earlier chapters of this book.

It should perhaps be made clear at the outset that in European Community Law, the principle of good administration is not always legally enforceable, as was pointed out by A.G. Slynn in Case 64/82 *Tradax v Commission*,[1] where he stated that he did not consider 'that there is any generalised principle of law that what is required by good administration will necessarily amount to a legally enforceable rule. To keep an efficient filing system may be an essential part of good administration but is not a legally enforceable rule. Legal rules and good administration may overlap (e.g. in the need to ensure fair play and proportionality); the requirements of the latter may be a factor in the elucidation of the former. The two are not necessarily synonymous. Indeed, sometimes when courts urge that something should be done as a matter of good administration, they do it because there is no precise legal rule'.

In many instances the conduct required of the Community administration is expressly laid down, and to that extent it is more easily susceptible to judicial review. One of these express requirements, that certain acts should be accompanied by a statement of reasons, will be considered more fully later in this chapter.

As a concluding general point, however, it should be borne in

[1.] [1984] ECR 1359 at pp. 1385–6.

mind that a breach even of an express requirement will not lead to the annulment of an act involving such a breach unless it can be shown that the resultant act would have been different had the breach not occurred,[2] so that where the Commission breached an express requirement not to communicate certain confidential information to the complainants in competition proceedings, it was held that this could not lead to the annulment of the subsequent decision since the information wrongly released had not enabled the complainant to put forward any argument likely to affect the substance of the decision.[3]

Turning to the principles of good administration developed by the European Court, these may be grouped for convenience under four main headings: administrative good faith, consistency, diligence, and communication.

Administrative good faith

This is a phrase frequently found in the judgments of the European Court. It seems to a certain extent to be equated with reasonableness, so that it was a breach of the principle for the Commission to leave Ireland five days in which to amend legislation which had been in force for some 40 years and with regard to which the Commission had made no previous complaint following Ireland's accession to the Community.[4] Similarly, in Case 293/85 *Commission v Belgium*,[5] the Commission allowed eight days to reply to its letter commencing enforcement proceedings under Article 169 of the EC Treaty, and 15 days to comply with a reasoned opinion requiring the elimination of certain fees charged to foreign students for university and vocational training courses. While the Court accepted that the fact that the academic year was about to start could justify short time limits, it took the view that in the circumstances of the case the Commission could have taken action during the previous six months and that therefore the urgency only arose because of the Commission's failure to take action earlier. The periods allowed were therefore not reasonable. On the other

2. Case 90/74 *Deboeck v Commission* [1975] ECR 1123.
3. Cases 209 to 215 and 218/78 *Van Landewyck v Commission* [1980] ECR 3125.
4. Case 74/82 *Commission v Ireland* [1984] ECR 317.
5. [1988] ECR 305.

hand, in Case C-56/90 *Commission v United Kingdom*[6] where the United Kingdom argued that it was physically impossible for it to adopt the necessary measures with regard to water quality within the two months laid down by the Commission in its reasoned opinion, the Court observed that the Commission had drawn the United Kingdom's attention to the situation almost two years before the reasoned opinion, so that the period allowed was reasonable. In any event, it was pointed out that one way of complying with the reasoned opinion would have been simply to prohibit bathing in the areas in question.[7] Obviously, there is a close link with the principle of proportionality, which, as noted in Chapter 3, first appeared in Community law in the context of the exercise of managerial discretion in Case 8/55 *Fédération Charbonnière de Belgique v High Authority*,[8] where it was held that the High Authority's reaction to illegal conduct must be in proportion. On the other hand, it has been held to be good administration for the Commission, where licences were available only for a limited quantity of goods, only to take account of those tenders which bid for the amount available or less, and to ignore those which bid for more than was available.[9]

Conversely, the principle of administrative good faith means that the Commission's conduct should be judged in the light of the information available to it at the relevant time rather than with the benefit of hindsight, so that in determining whether the Commission was justified in not taking protective measures against the import of certain potatoes, account should be taken of the information in its possession on the date when the decision was taken, and not of what happened on the market afterwards.[10]

The Community institutions are required to observe the principle of administrative good faith even when in dispute with their staff.[11] Thus, it was held to be contrary to 'the good faith which must govern relations between the Community administration and its officials' for the Commission to argue that actions were out of time as being in reality aimed at decisions concerning pension rights taken in 1978 when the officials concerned could not find out until individual calculations were made in 1981 how they

---

6. [1993] ECR I-4109.
7. Whatever the domestic consequences of prohibiting bathing at Blackpool.
8. [1954–56] ECR 292 at p. 299.
9. Case 354/87 *Weddel v Commission* [1990] ECR I-3847.
10. Case 114/83 *Société d'Initiatives v Commission* [1984] ECR 2589.
11. Cases 118 to 123/82 *Celant v Commission* [1983] ECR 2995.

would be affected by these decisions. Similarly, in Cases T-33/89 and T-74/89 *Blackman v European Parliament*,[12] it was held that the Parliament could not claim that the applicant was out of time in submitting his complaint under the Staff Regulations when, after telephoning the head of the welfare service for his advice, he had submitted his complaint in time to that service. It should have been submitted to the appointing authority, but instead of forwarding it to the appropriate department, the welfare service merely returned it to the applicant, with the result that he was late in submitting his complaint to the appointing authority.

On the other hand, it has been held to be incumbent upon a candidate for a post with one of the Community institutions to take steps to ensure that notices informing him of the date of tests will be able to reach him: in Case 155/85 *Strack v Parliament*[13] it was held that to give a candidate two weeks' notice of tests, even during the summer holidays, did not breach the principle of good administration.

Consistency

Another well-known general principle of Community law, the protection of legitimate expectation, discussed in Chapter 4, underlies the requirement that the Community institutions should behave in a consistent manner. In the area of management and administration, this is perhaps most clearly shown in Case 81/72 *Commission v Council*,[14] where it was held that a Decision taken by the Council on 21 March 1972 to apply for a period of three years a particular system of adjusting the salaries of Community staff had a binding effect so as to prevent the Council from validly adopting a Regulation which was not in accordance with its terms.

In the relationship between Community institutions and their staff, this rule is of particular importance with regard to what the European Court generically refers to as 'internal directives', measures internal to an institution which are not in themselves legally binding. Hence, the Commission's 'methods of procedure' for transferring officials from Grade B to Grade A, although they

---

12. [1993] II-ECR 249.
13. [1986] ECR 3561.
14. [1973] ECR 575. See Chapter 4 above.

did not constitute a rule of law binding on the administration, were held to be a rule of conduct indicating the practice to be followed, from which the administration could not depart without giving reasons.[15] This approach was held to be required also by the general principle of equality of treatment of the Commission's officials. In the result, a decision was annulled which departed from the 'methods of procedure' without giving reasons for so doing. A similar view has also been followed with regard, for example, to an 'internal directive' on the professional experience to be taken account of in grading officials under the Staff Regulations.[16]

At the institutional level, it has similarly been held that even in the context of the legislative process, internal rules must be followed. So, in Case 68/86 *United Kingdom v Council* [17] it was held that while previous practice of the Council could not alter the voting majorities required by the provisions of the Treaty, its internal rules could lay down the mechanisms for determining which voting procedure should be used, and could therefore require unanimous agreement before the written procedure was used, even if the substantive vote would be by qualified majority. Therefore, if the Council's rules of procedure did lay down such a requirement, those rules must be followed unless the Council formally modified them.

Moving away from internal rules, there is one well-known case where the exercise of the Commission's managerial discretion, in this case as to whether or not to institute proceedings under Article 169 of the EC Treaty, appears to have had a quasi-legislative effect. This is the *Defrenne*[18] case, where the Court held that the direct effect of Article 119 of the EC Treaty on equal pay for equal work as between men and women could only be invoked from the date of its judgment rather than from 1962, when it should have been implemented. The crux of the matter is a statement by the Court that 'in the light of the conduct of several of the Member States and the views adopted by the Commission and repeatedly brought to the notice of the circles concerned, it was appropriate

---

15. Cases 80–83/81 and 182–185/82 *Adams and others v Commission* [1984] ECR 3411.
16. Case 25/83 *Buick v Commission* [1984] ECR 1773; Case 343/82 *Michael v Commission* [1983] ECR 4023; Case 190/82 *Blomefield v Commission* [1983] ECR 3981. In these cases the internal directive was in fact interpreted against the applicants.
17. [1988] ECR 855.
18. Case 43/75 *Defrenne v Sabena* [1976] ECR 455.

to take exceptionally into account the fact that over a prolonged period the parties concerned had been led to continue with practices which are contrary to Article 119'. In particular, the Court took account of the fact that although the Commission from time to time had threatened to institute proceedings under Article 169 of the EC Treaty, for breach of Treaty obligations, it did not in fact do so. This was likely to consolidate an incorrect impression as to the effects of Article 119. Although it does not recognise that the Court is creating new law, this appears to be recognising a kind of estoppel on a point of law, preventing the law being invoked for the past. This, to say the least, seems an interesting innovation, all the more interesting since the Court had held that a resolution of the Member States of 30 December 1961 and Council Directive 75/117 could not prejudice the direct effect of Article 119 at the expiry of the time limits laid down under it and under the Act of Accession – yet the Commission's conduct could! The obvious question is, how can an institution by its conduct produce a result which could not produce by express legislation? Be that as it may, it should be observed that the Court also grounded its judgment on the general principle of legal certainty.[19]

By way of contrast, there are many cases where it has been held that an individual may not rely on the wrongful conduct of the Commission, as in Case 188/82 *Thyssen*,[20] where a steel undertaking which had been unable to use the full tolerance on its quota for the last quarter of 1980, because it was communicated too late by the Commission, thereupon exceeded its quota for the first quarter of 1981. The European Court quite simply stated that 'a wrongful act on the part of the Commission cannot justify a breach of Community law by an undertaking, regardless of the economic justification relied on by the latter', although it did reduce the fine imposed to the symbolic level of 5 ecu. Similarly, an individual cannot claim the benefit of illegal conduct which has been extended to others in the past: in Case 188/83 *Witte v European Parliament*[21] the applicant tried unsuccessfully to invoke the benefit of the previous administrative practice of the Community institutions of treating an absence of six months during the previous five years from the place of employment as justifying an expatriation allow-

---

19. See Chapter 4 above.
20. [1983] ECR 3721.
21. [1984] ECR 3465.

ance and of treating the children of expatriate officials taking employment with an institution as if they were themselves expatriates. These practices hardly accorded with the wording of the Staff regulations, and have been terminated following criticism by the Court of Auditors.

A similar approach has been taken with regard to past practices in the legislative process. In Case 68/86 *United Kingdom v Council*, [22] in the context of a Directive enacted under agricultural provisions of the Treaty which was admitted by the Council to deal also with the harmonisation of national laws with a view to the protection of consumers and public health, the United Kingdom invoked the fact that the previous practice of the Council when faced with such mixed objectives had been to use a dual legal basis, making reference also to the general Article 100 of the Treaty. It was held, however, that the legal basis must rest on objective factors which are amenable to judicial review, and that a mere practice on the part of the Council could not derogate from the rules laid down in the Treaty and could not create a precedent binding on Community institutions with regard to the correct legal basis.

It is also well established that no Community official can give a valid undertaking not to apply Community law,[23] and in one of the cases arising under the ECSC steel production quota system,[24] the Court held that the Commission is not bound by a statement of one of its senior officials promising that a fine will not be imposed; while that particular case also turned on the point that the Commission had no discretion but to impose a fine if a breach of the production quota was established, it appears to fall into the same category as the decision in a competition case,[25] holding that the view of a senior official that an agreement is capable of exemption could not bind the Commission. On the other hand, in Cases 29, 31, 36, 39–47, 50 and 51/63 *Usines de la Providence v High Authority*,[26] where promises to pay a 'transport parity' were made consistently over a period of time by officials of the old ECSC High Authority, this was held to constitute a lack of care by the High Authority in supervising its officials, so that although the

---

[22]. [1988] ECR 855.
[23]. Case 188/82 *Thyssen v Commission* [1983] ECR 3721.
[24]. Cases 303 and 312/81 *Klöckner-Werke v Commission* [1983] ECR 1599.
[25]. Case 71/74 *FRUBO v Commission* [1975] ECR 563.
[26]. [1965] ECR 911.

'transport parities' as such could not be paid, the High Authority was liable in damages.

There is, however, one area where it is clear that traders may not rely even on the previous *lawful* conduct of the Commission itself. This is with regard to the level of fines which may be imposed for breaches of the EC competition rules. In the *Pioneer* case,[27] for example, the European Court held that the Commission was not bound to mention in the statement of objections the possibility of a change in its policy regarding the general level of fines, since this was a matter of general policy unrelated to the facts of the particular case. Indeed, later in the judgment, after mentioning that the Commission had admitted that it had in this case imposed a level of fines considerably higher than in the past, the court stated that not only is the Commission not estopped from raising the level of fines for certain types of infringement, but that 'the proper application of the Community competition rules requires that the Commission may at any time adjust the level of fines to the needs of that policy'. Whatever may be thought of this principle by the undertakings affected, it does seem to accord with the established case-law on the subject. Thus, in the *BMW* cases,[28] it was held that the fact that the Commission had not previously seen fit to fine retailers in the type of situation at issue did not prevent it from exercising its power to do so. On the other hand, although reliance may not be placed upon the Commission's practice with regard to the level of fines, it is clear that before a penalty may be imposed at all, there must be a clear and unambiguous provision authorising its imposition.

Diligence

The principle of diligence in Community administration is here used to cover, in particular, the duty to reply to requests and to act in due time. Some time-limits for the performance of such obligations are stated expressly in the Treaties: Article 175 of the EC Treaty and Article 35 of the ECSC Treaty set a period of two months during which the Commission (or Council under the EC Treaty) may respectively define its position or act to avoid an ac-

---

[27.] Cases 100–103/80 *Pioneer v Commission* [1983] ECR 1825.
[28.] Cases 32/78 and 36–82/78 *BMW v Commission* [1979] ECR 2435.

tion for failure to act. This time-limit has been applied by analogy to the Commission's consideration of State aids,[29] where it has been held that a new aid which had been notified to the Commission by a Member State under Article 93 of the EC Treaty should be treated as an 'existing' aid (and therefore not requiring approval in advance from the Commission) if the Commission did not respond within two months, on the basis that the Commission could not be regarded as acting with 'proper diligence' if it omitted to define its attitude within a reasonable period. However, although the Commission was not therefore bound to take a formal favourable decision, the Court did add that 'it is in the interests of good administration for the Commission ... to inform the State concerned' – an example of the requirement of communication to be considered later in this chapter.

Perhaps the most extreme example of failure to reply to complaints has occurred in relation to staff disputes. Under Articles 90 and 91 of the Staff Regulations, an official of a Community institution must submit a complaint through his immediate superior to his appointing authority, which has four months to respond, before bringing an action; this system was intended to reduce the number of staff cases coming before the European Court by allowing an internal remedy, but there have been periods where the obligation to respond appears to have been virtually ignored by the institutions. It was recorded in the House of Lords Select Committee's Report on the abortive 1979 proposal to establish an EC Staff Administrative Tribunal[30] that of 15 staff cases decided by the Court in 1978, in only one case had a full reply been made to the internal complaint within the time-limit!

Even where no specific time-limit is laid down or no express obligation to reply is imposed, the Court has adopted a general principle that the institutions should reply to requests. Two examples may be given of a failure to reply on the part of the Commission which gave rise to the comments of the Court. In the *IAZ International* case,[31] in the context of an alleged breach of Article 85 of the EC Treaty, the Court held that the Commission had failed to observe the requirements of good administration by failing to respond to a draft of a revised agreement between the parties con-

---

29. Case 120/73 *Lorenz v Germany* [1973] ECR 1471.
30. Session 1978–9, 17th Report.
31. Cases 96–102, 104, 105, 108 and 110/82, [1983] ECR 3369.

cerned, even if that revised agreement did not meet all the points raised by the Commission and could not have altered the ultimate decision. In the *Lucchini* case,[32] the Commission failed to reply to a telex from a steel undertaking offering to cut its future production so as to make up for having previously exceeded its production quota. In this latter case, the Commission's conduct led the Court to reduce the fine imposed on the undertaking concerned to half the normal rate. Fines have similarly been reduced where the Commission did not respond to a request for the alteration of a steel delivery quota until the quota in question had expired,[33] and a symbolic fine has been imposed where a revised quota was communicated late by the Commission.[34]

More generally, the Commission has been ordered to pay an official's costs where there was undue delay in indicating his administrative position,[35] and in Case 19/69 *Richez-Parise*[36] the European Court held that although the giving of wrong information to an official did not in itself give rise to liability in damages, delay in rectifying that information did give rise to liability. A similar view has been taken where officials were misled as to the very existence of a rent allowance; it was held that in so far as the error was not corrected in good time, as a result of negligence on the part of the Commission, the applicants could recover damages to compensate for the harm suffered as a result of the Commission's maladministration.[37]

On the other hand, there are some instances where the European Court has not regarded apparently quite lengthy delays as breaching the principles of good administration. So, in Case 103/83 *Usinor v Commission*,[38] a delay of 18 months in adapting ECSC quotas to meet the demand for certain new products, from when the Commission's attention was drawn to the point, was held not to be excessive, presumably because of the need to investigate the situation. Also, in Case 14/78 *Denkavit v Commission*,[39] a delay of 21 months before the Commission commenced enforcement proceedings against Italy under Article 169 of the EC Treaty

32. Case 179/82, [1983] ECR 3083.
33. Case 2/83 *Alfer v Commission* [1984] ECR 799.
34. Case 188/82 *Thyssen v Commission* [1983] ECR 3721.
35. Case 61/74 *Santopietro v Commission* [1975] ECR 483.
36. Case 19/69, [1970] ECR 325.
37. Cases 176 and 177/86 *Houyoux v Commission* [1987] ECR 4333.
38. [1984] ECR 3483.
39. [1978] ECR 2497.

in relation to an Italian prohibition of certain substances in animal foodstuffs was accepted on the grounds that 'the Commission cannot be blamed for having waited until it was fully informed before adopting a decision in a matter as complex as the presence in feeding-stuffs of substances which might prove to be undesirable from the point of view of human or animal health'. It would appear, therefore, that the greater the technical complexity of the matter, the greater the delay that is acceptable – though the commentator might be forgiven for doubting whether the assessment of the compatibility of a State aid with Community law could always be regarded as a non-complex problem, despite the mere two months allowed in *Lorenz*.[40] However, the Court of First Instance has held that a delay of three years in preparing a report is a 'faute de service' if it leaves an official's file irregular or incomplete, giving rise to a liability in damages.[41]

Communication

There is a sense in which communication can be regarded as an aspect of the duty of diligence. When the Commission sent a letter containing important information with regard to an anti-dumping procedure by ordinary post rather than by registered post, with the result that it could not be established with absolute certainty that it had been received by the addressee, it was held that this could not be regarded as a diligent method of discharging the obligation to provide information laid down in the basic anti-dumping regulation.[42]

It is now well established in Community law that communication of a decision is separate from the taking of that decision. So far as Community officials are concerned, Article 25 of the Staff Regulations requires decisions relating to specific individuals to be communicated in writing to the official concerned, but in Cases 316/82 and 40/83 *Kohler v Court of Auditors*[43] it was held that since communication necessarily follows the making of a deci-

---

40. [1973] ECR 1471.
41. Case T-73/89 *Barbi* [1990] ECR II-619.
42. Case C-49/88 *Al-Jubail Fertilizer v Commission* [1991] ECR I-3187 at p. 3242.
43. [1984] ECR 641.

sion,[44] written communication could not be a pre-condition for the existence of a decision; that case in fact involved an oral decision communicated in a conversation between the President of the Court of Auditors and the applicant, and the Court of Justice took the view that, in any event, it was not open to the Court of Auditors to claim that its own failure to communicate the decision in writing meant that there was no decision. However, this also means that delay in communicating a decision will not lead to the annulment of the decision as such, since communication, being later in time, can have no influence on the substance of the decision. However, in the case[45] in which this point arose, which involved delay by the European Parliament, the delay was said to be 'regrettable', and the Parliament was ordered to pay the costs; it continues to be the case that a failure to communicate information may lead to the institution being required to pay the costs or a proportion of them.[46]

To some extent, the degree of communication required by Community principles of good administration may overlap with principles of natural justice. Under Article 26 of the Staff Regulations, documents concerning administrative status, and all reports relating to ability, efficiency and conduct may not be used or cited by the institutions *against* an official unless they were communicated to him before they were filed. A similar approach has been developed by case-law in relation to competition proceedings before the Commission, so that the Commission may not rely on undisclosed information in reaching its decision.[47] Hence, if the Commission wishes to protect its sources, or is not allowed to pass on certain information (e.g. business secrets), it cannot make direct use of that information.

Three particular problems will next be considered which, if they are not concerned with the mechanical process of communication, can nevertheless be regarded as concerned with communication in a broader sense: the duty not to mislead, the liability to explain and the duty to state reasons.

[44.] As previously held in Case 125/80 *Arning v Commission* [1981] ECR 2539 at p. 2552.

[45.] Case 111/83 *Picciolo v European Parliament* [1984] ECR 4249.

[46.] See the judgment of the Court of First Instance in Case T-156/89 *Mordt* [1991] ECR II-407.

[47.] Case 322/81 *Michelin v Commission* [1983] ECR 3461; Case 107/82 *AEG Telefunken v Commission* [1983] ECR 3157.

Duty not to mislead

The principle that there may be a liability in damages where loss has been suffered as a result of giving of misleading information by a Community institution was established in Case 169/73 *Continentale France v Council*,[48] although, as was noted in Chapter 4, it was there held that the applicant, as a prudent trader knowing the market, should not have relied on the Council's information. The basic criterion of liability appears to be whether the conduct in question 'could and should have caused such an error in the mind of a prudent person'. At first sight this is difficult to reconcile with the cases mentioned above, where liability was held to flow not from the giving of wrong information but from the failure of the institution adequately to supervise its officials[49] or from its failure to correct the wrongful information.[50] The difference may well be that in this case the information purported to be issued by the Council as an institution for the information of third parties.

In a number of cases, the giving of misleading information by an official has been reflected in the order as to costs. Hence, in Cases 15 and 29/59 *Knutange v HA*,[51] the successful defendant was ordered to pay the costs of an action caused by the receipt of a letter from a High Authority official implying that a decision had been taken when that was not the case. Similarly,[52] the Commission was ordered to pay the costs where a senior Commission official had given the applicant incorrect information regarding expatriation allowances, and the same occurred[53] where the applicants had been given incorrect information with regard to the exchange rates at which they could transfer some of their salary to their home State.

Liability to explain

Apart from the express requirement to state reasons for most Community acts, the European Court has, as a matter of case-law, developed a general principle that explanations should be given, particularly where an individual or trader is treated other-

---

48. [1975] ECR 117.
49. *Usines de la Providence*, see note 39 above.
50. *Richez-Parise*, see note 37 above.
51. [1960] ECR 1.
52. Case 137/79 *Kohll v Commission* [1980] ECR 2601.
53. Cases 783 and 786/79 *Venus and Obert v Commission* [1981] ECR 2445.

wise than he might normally expect to be treated under general Community law. In practice, this often means that the institution is required to state how it has acted, as well as why it has acted. In Case 144/82 *Detti v Court of Justice*,[54] the Court's selection board had failed to indicate the criteria by which it had marked the papers of candidates taking a test in Luxembourg more severely than the papers of candidates taking the same test in Brussels (apparently because the candidates in Brussels had accidentally been given a longer dictation passage). The Court in its judicial capacity therefore annulled the decision of its selection board, on the basis that a corrective factor must be applied unequivocally and that the persons concerned were entitled to be informed of the criteria adopted. On the other hand,[55] it has been held that a failure to indicate the conditions required for the recruitment of all candidates under the exceptional procedure of Article 29(2) of the Staff Regulations,[56] so that the normal rules would not in any event apply, did not automatically invalidate the selection made, although even here it could give rise to a liability in damages, and the Parliament (the defendant institution) was ordered to pay the costs.

In the steel sector, it was held in Case 270/82 *Estel v Commission*[57] that the Commission should have communicated the methods by which it had altered steel quotas, although the only outcome here was that the Court reduced the fine for exceeding the quota.

The problem also arises in connection with the calculation of prices in agricultural markets where general legislation may be at issue. In Case 64/82 *Tradax v Commission*,[58] the Court did lay down criteria as to when the Commission may be required to explain its calculations. It held that the Commission could be required to produce its calculation of CIF prices of cereals (which were at issue in that case) in judicial proceedings, but that as a matter of 'good administration' it should also periodically publish the data used. However, it was not required to publish the data on the request of an individual trader. It would therefore appear that, as will be evident with regard to the express requirement to state

---

54. [1983] ECR 2421.
55. Case 289/81 *Mavrides v European Parliament* [1983] ECR 1731.
56. Which allows a procedure other than the competition procedure to be used for the recruitment of Grade A1 or A2 officials.
57. [1984] ECR 1195.
58. [1984] ECR 1359.

reasons, less explanation is required of general legislation than is required where an act is addressed to an individual.

Duty to state reasons

Article 190 of the EC Treaty stipulates that 'Regulations, Directives and Decisions adopted jointly by the European Parliament and the Council, and such acts adopted by the Council or the Commission, shall state the reasons on which they are based and shall refer to any proposals or opinions which were required to be obtained pursuant to this Treaty', i.e. it lays down the requirement that those acts which are defined in the Treaties as being capable of producing binding effects must be reasoned. The ECSC Treaty, on the other hand, also requires that Opinions, which are defined as having no binding force, should be reasoned, its Article 15 laying down that 'Decisions, Recommendations and Opinions of the Commission shall state the reasons on which they are based ...'; indeed, even under the system of the EC and the Euratom Treaties, individual provisions of those Treaties authorising Opinions to be issued do in fact tend to require them to be reasoned. Hence, under Article 169 of the EC Treaty, if the Commission considers that a Member States has failed to fulfil an obligation under that Treaty, it delivers a 'reasoned opinion' on the matter.

It is clear that the extent of the obligation to state reasons depends on the nature of the measure in question and on the context in which it was adopted.[59] With regard to acts which are general in nature, it has been held that the statement of reasons 'may be confined to indicating the general situation which led to its adoption, on the one hand, and the general objectives which it is intended to achieve on the other'.[60] With regard to the role of the statement of reasons in decisions which are individual in nature and which are therefore more relevant to discussion of managerial or administrative discretion, the Court enounced the view which it has subsequently maintained most clearly in Case 24/62 *Germany v Commission*,[61] where it held that Article 190 of the EC Treaty 'seeks to give an opportunity to the parties of defending their rights, to the Court of exercising its supervisory functions, and to

[59] See e.g. Case 32/86 *Sisma v Commission* [1987] ECR 1645 at para. 8, Case C-189/90 *Cipeke v Commission* [1992] ECR I-3573 at para. 14.

[60] Case 5/67 *Beus v HZA München* [1968] ECR 83.

[61] [1963] ECR 63.

Member States and to all interested nationals of ascertaining the circumstances in which the Commission has applied the Treaty. To obtain these objectives, it is sufficient for the Decision to set out, in a concise but clear and relevant manner, the principal issues of law and fact upon which it is based and which are necessary in order that the reasoning which has led the Commission to its Decision may be understood'. So defined, the statement of reasons has become an extremely important element in the development of judicial control over individual decisions: it forces the institution to commit itself as to what are the relevant issues of law and fact, and in so doing gives those affected something concrete to challenge, if they are so minded, and gives the Court something concrete to review. Indeed, it may be observed that the Commission's individual competition decisions consist largely of a statement of reasons, with only a few lines of substantive decision at the end.

Leaving aside the steel sector, and the EC competition rules, it will be evident from the earlier part of this chapter that it is in their dealings with their officials that the Community institutions act in a manner which is most clearly administrative or managerial and it is here that the requirement for a statement of reasons has been more restrictively interpreted in the context of individual decisions, although a trend towards greater judicial control would appear to be evolving. Under Article 25 of the Staff Regulations, 'any decision relating to a specific individual which is taken under these Staff Regulations shall at once be communicated in writing to the official concerned. Any decision *adversely affecting* an official shall state the grounds on which it is based'. The relationship of this provision to the basic Treaty requirements does not always appear to have been considered, although it should be borne in mind that the Treaty requirements are expressed to apply only to the joint acts of the Parliament and Council and to the Council and Commission (in the case of the ECSC only the Commission) and not the other institutions.

Before the enactment of the Staff Regulations, it was held, apparently as an application of a general principle of administrative law, in Cases 43, 45 and 48/59 *Lachmuller v Commission*,[62] that a statement of the grounds for a decision affecting an official must be made in terms which are specific and capable of being challenged. Since its enactment, however, Article 25 of the Staff Regu-

---

62. [1960] ECR 463 at pp. 474–5.

lations has tended to be taken very much at face value: so, in a line of cases beginning with Cases 94 and 96/63 *Bernusset v Commission*,[63] it has been held that there is no need for a decision promoting an individual to be reasoned since it does not adversely affect the person to whom it is addressed, i.e. the successful candidate, and that to give reasons for not appointing the unsuccessful candidates might prejudice them. However, since the judgment in Case 44/71 *Marcato v Commission*,[64] this position has been relaxed somewhat in so far as an appointment or promotion results from a competition: although the final choice need not be reasoned, it was held that there was a first stage during which it was decided whether the candidates complied with the conditions set out in the notice of competition and hence could be allowed to take part in the competition. The Court found that this was carried out on the basis of information which was objective, and that 'sufficient reasons must be given for the reasons arrived at'. It was held not to be sufficient simply to indicate the condition the applicant was considered not to satisfy, without explaining why. This view has been repeated, e.g. in Case 112/78 *Sonne v Commission*.[65] Here, the applicant had been admitted to take part in a competition in 1975, but was refused admission to a competition for which similar qualifications were required in 1977. The Second Chamber held that 'a candidate cannot form the subject of a less favourable appraisal than that made of him in a previous competition, unless the statement of reasons on which the decision is based clearly justifies such a difference of appraisal', and that a mere reference to the condition which was not fulfilled could not satisfy this requirement.

However, by way of contrast, in Case 69/83 *Lux v Court of Auditors*,[66] the Second Chamber held that account could be taken of the surrounding circumstances (including previous conduct) to see if a decision was adequately reasoned, even if the express reasoning was not sufficient in itself. In its context, the decision was held to be adequately reasoned, although the Court of Auditors was ordered to pay the costs since the litigation was caused by the inadequacy of its express reasoning. Outside the context of staff disputes, it may be observed that the Court and the Court of First

---

[63.] [1964] ECR 297 at p. 309.
[64.] [1972] ECR 427 at p. 434.
[65.] [1979] ECR 1573.
[66.] [1984] ECR 2447.

Instance have subsequently held that account should be taken of the context in determining the adequacy of a statement of reasons in areas as diverse as exemptions from customs duties[67] and withdrawal of vocational training funds under the European Social Fund.[68]

Furthermore, the Court has stated on a number of occasions that an internal measure which does not affect the statutory position of an official need not be reasoned,[69] even though it may adversely affect the personal position of the official, as when scientists from a Euratom research centre were refused permission to present papers at an international conference.[70]

Perhaps the lowest point in the Court's view of the role of the statement of reasons in staff cases was reached in relation to dismissals under Article 50 of the Staff Regulations. Most of the provisions concerned with dismissal specifically required a reasoned decision, but Article 50, which allows for the 'retirement' by the appointing authority of certain very senior officials (in grades A1 or A2) 'in the interests of the service' does not. Thus, in Case 17/68 *Reinarz v Commission*,[71] the First Chamber of the Court held that 'it is clear from this provision that reasons do not have to be given for such decisions'! However, in Case 34/77 *Oslizlok v Commission*,[72] when the matter again came before the First Chamber, it was held that a statement that the comparative qualifications of the various officials concerned had actually been examined satisfied 'the requirements contained in Article 190 of the Treaty and the second paragraph of Article 25 of the Staff Regulations to the effect that decisions shall state the reasons on which they are based'. Thus, it would appear that there is, albeit to a very limited degree, some recognition of the Treaty requirements even in the matter of decisions affecting officials.

Such requirements do not, however, appear to have been followed in certain cases concerned with dismissals at the other end of the spectrum. In Case 346/82 *Favre v Commission*[73] it was held that there was no need to communicate the reasons for the dis-

---

67. Case 185/83 *University of Groningen v Inspecteur der Invoerrechten en Accijnzen* [1984] ECR 3623.
68. Case T-81/95 *Interhotel v Commission* (14 July 1997).
69. Cases 36, 37 and 218/81 *Seton v Commission* [1983] ECR 1789.
70. Case 338/82 *Albertini and Montagnani v Commission* [1984] ECR 2123.
71. [1969] ECR 61 at p. 70.
72. [1978] ECR 1099 at p. 1114.
73. [1984] ECR 2269.

missal of a probationary temporary official on an indeterminate contract under Article 47(2)(a) of the 'Conditions of Employment of Other Servants of the European Communities', on the basis that that provision empowered the employing institution to terminate a contract simply on giving the appropriate period of notice, so that the Court could not intervene unless there was a patent error or misuse of power.[74] While, from the reports of these cases it would appear that the officials concerned can have had little doubt as to why they were dismissed, the judgments hardly seem to accord with the principle that the decision itself should be reasoned underlying Article 190 of the Treaty and Article 25 of the Staff Regulations.

Effects of failure to observe rules of good administration

The range of remedies available will have appeared from the discussion of the principles of good administration. A summary may, however, be attempted here. Where the rule of good administration is one expressly laid down by Community law, such as the requirement to state reasons, its breach may well constitute an infringement of the Treaties or of any rule of law relating to their application or an infringement of an essential procedural requirement, so as to lead to the annulment of an act resulting from or involving such a breach, under Article 173 of the EC Treaty or Article 33 of the ECSC Treaty, or a declaration of invalidity on a reference for a preliminary ruling. However, it has also been seen that breach of unwritten general principles of good administration may also lead to annulment, as where 'methods of procedure' were not followed[75] or where corrective factors applied to recruitment lists were not indicated,[76] or where legitimate expectations were breached.[77]

There is indeed some authority for the view that an act not susceptible to annulment may nevertheless be declared 'inexistent'. In

---

74. The fact that a temporary official is employed under a contract marks a fundamental distinction from an established official, who is employed under the terms of the Staff Regulations.

75. Cases 80-83/81 and 182-185/82 *Adam v Commission* [1984] ECR 3411.

76. Case 144/82 *Detti v Court of Justice* [1983] ECR 2421.

77. Case 81/72 *Commission v Council* [1973] ECR 575.

Case 1 and 14/57 *Usines a Tubes de la Sarre v HA*[78] the Court was faced with an application for the annulment of what purported to be an Opinion under Article 54 of the ECSC Treaty; in considering the real nature of this act, it was held that a statement of reasons for an Opinion was not only required by the ECSC Treaty, but that 'it is an essential, indeed constituent element of such an act, with the result that in the absence of a statement of reasons that act cannot exist', and the Court concluded that the measure at issue, not being reasoned, was non-existent! This doctrine of 'non-existence' may not be totally unconnected with the fact that, as the Court itself recognised later in its judgment, under Article 33 of the ECSC Treaty it has jurisdiction to annul only Decisions and Recommendations, and not Opinions; hence by declaring the measure 'non-existent' it was exercising control over an act which it has no direct power to annul. Following the hint thrown out by the Court in its judgment in Case 60/81 *IBM v Commission*[79] that mere procedural steps not in themselves acts capable of annulment may nonetheless be subject to judicial review 'where the measures concerned lack even the appearance of legality', it may be wondered if the declaration of 'inexistence' would be appropriate here also.

The payment of damages may also be ordered where harm results from a failure to observe the requirements of good administration, such as a lack of supervision or control of the statements made by officials to undertakings,[80] or undue delay in rectifying incorrect information,[81] and it would appear from Case 289/81 *Mavrides v European Parliament*[82] that damages may be the appropriate remedy where the failure at issue is not of such a nature as automatically to invalidate the measure in question. The principles of good administration may also be used as a defence as in Cases 118-123/82 *Celant v Commission*,[83] where the requirement of administrative good faith was invoked to resist a claim by the Commission that the action was out of time.

In many cases, a breach of the requirements of good administration has led to a reduction in the level of a fine imposed by the

---

78. [1957 and 1958] ECR 105 at pp. 112–13.
79. [1981] ECR 2639.
80. Cases 29, 31, 36, 39–47, 50 and 51/63 *Usines de la Providence v HA* [1965] ECR 911.
81. Case 19/69 *Richez-Parise v Commission* [1970] ECR 325.
82. [1983] ECR 1731. 83. [1983] ECR 2925.

Commission, if not to the annulment of the decision as such, as in several cases involving failure or delay by the Commission in responding to requests for alteration of ECSC quotas.[84]

Finally, it may be observed that in many cases where the failure on the part of an EC institution to observe the principles of good administration does not in itself affect the legality of what has been done, that institution may still be ordered to meet the costs, as where the applicant has been misled by the drafting of the measure at issue[85] or there has been a failure to communicate relevant information.[86]. In a number of instances, however, the recognition that the standards of good administration have not been observed is accompanied by nothing more than an expression of regret on the part of the Court, particularly, it might be said, in matters of competition procedure.[87] For the most part, this can perhaps best be explained as an illustration of the general principles that a breach of Community law will only successfully ground an action for annulment if it can be shown that the act at issue would have been different in the absence of the irregularity[88] and that the applicant has an interest in taking the point.[89]

Although the pattern is not wholly uniform, it may certainly be stated by way of conclusion that, in the context of administration as opposed to legislation, while not every breach of the principles of 'good administration' may give rise to legal remedies, a legal remedy is available in Community Law if that breach affects a legal or legally protected situation or gives rise to quantifiable harm.

[84.] See e.g. Case 188/82 *Thyssen v Commission* [1983] ECR 3721.

[85.] See e.g. Case 25/83 *Buick v Commission* [1984] ECR 1773; Case T-7/90 *Kobor* [1990] ECR II-721.

[86.] See e.g. Case 289/81 *Mavrides* [1983] ECR 1731.

[87.] See e.g. Cases 96–102, 104, 105, 108 and 110/82 *IAZ International v Commission* [1983] ECR 3369.

[88.] See e.g. Cases 209–215 and 218/78 *Van Landewyck v Commission* [1980] ECR 3125 at p. 3239.

[89.] Case 90/74 *Deboeck v Commission* [1975] ECR 1123. See Usher, *European Court Practice* (Sweet and Maxwell, London 1983) paras. 1–32.

CHAPTER EIGHT

Status and use of general principles of Community law

Introduction

It will be apparent from the previous chapter that not all general principles of Community law have the same status, and that breach of them does not necessarily have the same legal consequences. An express recognition of this is to be found in the judgment of the Full Court in Case C-353/92 *Greece v Commission*[1] where, following a claim by the Greek government that a provision in a Regulation placed Community soya bean producers in a less competitive position than producers in non-Member States, the Court adopted the view of A.G. Jacobs that Community preference was not in any case a legal requirement the violation of which would result in the invalidity of the measure concerned. It will nevertheless be recalled that, at the national level, that selfsame principle has been held to require Member States to impose certain charges on goods imported from third countries which breach the effective uniformity of the Common Customs Tariff.[2]

Subject to this caveat, the aim of this chapter is to examine how general principles of Community law have been used as an aid to interpretation, as a criterion of the validity of Community legislation, as a basis for the award of damages against Community institutions, and as a constraint on the activities of Member States.

[1.] [1994] ECR I-3411 at p. 3451.
[2.] See Chapter 2, p. 15 above.

Interpretation

Perhaps the most obvious use of a general principle of Community law as an aid to interpretation is the use of the general principle of legal certainty to hold that the view set out in a particular judgment will only apply from the date of that judgment, which was discussed in Chapter 4. However, it may be asserted in more general terms that the most frequent use of these general principles is as a guide to interpretation, so as to ensure the validity of that legislation, rather than as a criterion for determining the validity of that legislation. The general principle of legal certainty was so used in the *Deuka* cases.[3] In the first of these the Court was asked whether a Commission Regulation was invalid in so far as it provided that an increased denaturing premium should be discontinued even in respect of wheat purchased by the denaturer before the Regulation came into force. Having found that a denaturing undertaking may well arrange its programme on the basis of an entire crop year, for the sake of legal certainty the Regulation had to be applied in such a way that there might still benefit from the system those quantities of goods purchased before the coming into force of the Regulation, provided the request (for a premium) was made to the intervention agency before the expiry of the time-limit arising from the Regulation. Interpreted in this way, the Regulation was held to be valid. In the second case, similar questions arose concerning the validity of Regulations respectively reducing and abolishing the relevant denaturing premium, and a similar answer was given: the Court stated that where there had been a commitment to denaturing before the expiry of the periods stipulated in the Regulations, it was right to apply, in the interests of legal certainty, for the computation of the amount of the denaturing premium, the provisions in force at the time the application was lodged, even if the technical mixing was not done until a subsequent date.

General principles of Community law may also be used in conjunction with the techniques of interpretation as such used by the Court, such as purposive or teleological interpretation or its cautious willingness to apply legislation by analogy to situations not falling within its precise terms. Interpretation by analogy has

---

3. Case 78/74 *Deuka v Einfuhr- und Vorratsstelle Getreide* [1975] ECR 421; Case 5/75 *Deuka v Einfuhr- und Vorratsstelle Getreide* [1975] ECR 759.

therefore been used to remedy a breach of a general principle, so that when, in Case 165/84 *Krohn*[4] it was held to be a breach of the principle of equality of treatment not to allow importers of manioc from Thailand to cancel their licences when importers from other third countries could do so, the Court held that the parallel legislation governing imports from countries other than Thailand should be applied by analogy to imports from Thailand.

Application of legislation by analogy has also been used to prevent a breach of a general principle: in Cases 201 and 202/85 *Klensch v Luxembourg Minister of Agriculture,*[5] it was decided that where Council Regulation 857/84 did not provide expressly for the reallocation of the milk-quota of a farmer who left dairy farming of his own volition, the rules which would have applied if he had left dairy farming under the special outgoers' scheme should apply by analogy, so that his quota should go to the national reserve. To allocate his quota to the purchaser to which he had made his deliveries, as the Luxembourg government had done, would in the Court's view, breach the principle of non-discrimination with regard to other producers, and would tie that producer to the one purchaser if he wanted to re-enter the market.

Criterion of validity

While breach of the principle of Community preference may not lead to the invalidity of the measure at issue,[6] it will be clear from the earlier part of this book that breaches of the principles of, for example, non-discrimination, proportionality, legitimate expectation, and the right to be heard may lead to the invalidity of a Community act.

Questions of validity may be raised before the Court (or Court of First Instance, as the case may be) in an action for annulment, a plea of illegality relating to direct action before the Court, a reference from a national court, or in the context of a claim. This last aspect will be considered in the next section of this chapter, but the underlying problem is to determine how the Court may take account of general principles in these different heads of jurisdiction.

[4.] [1985] ECR 3997.
[5.] [1986] ECR 3477.
[6.] Case C-353/92 *Greece v Commission* [1994] ECR I-3411 at p. 3451.

Actions for annulment

The same four grounds for annulment are recognised under all three Treaties: lack of competence; infringement of an essential procedural requirement; infringement of the Treaty or of any rule of law relating to its application; and misuse of powers.

The right to be heard, which was held to be breached in Case 17/74 *Transocean v Commission*,[7] was a requirement not laid down by the EC Treaty or by the relevant secondary legislation. However, having accepted the existence of this general rule, the Court then said that breach of the rule would be regarded as a breach of an essential procedural requirement under Article 173 of the Treaty, and annulled the condition at issue. This concept has broadened, so that it might be said, after Case C-49/88 *Al-Jubail Fertiliser v Council*,[8] that a failure to respect fundamental rights recognised in Community law will amount to a breach of an essential procedural requirement; in that case, as has been noted, the Commission could not show that the applicants had received the information necessary to be able to put their case in anti-dumping proceedings against them.

On the other hand, in Case C-135/92 *Fiskano v Commission*,[9] where the Commission had indicated that it would refuse to grant a fishing licence for a boat owned by the applicant, without having given the applicant an opportunity to put its point of view, the letter at issue was annulled simply on the ground that it breached the right to be heard, without reference to the terminology of Article 173.

Be that as it may, it has long been established that a breach of a general principle may be regarded as a breach of the Treaty itself. In Case 112/77 *Töpfer v Commission*[10] the applicant, who held a large number of licences for the export of white sugar issued before 26 April 1977 in respect of which customs export formalities were effected after 15 July 1977, brought an action under Article 173 for the annulment of a Commission Regulation which had the effect of reducing the compensation payable in DM to holders of sugar export licences issued before 26 April 1977 with effect from 15 July 1977. The applicant claimed, *inter alia*, that the regulation

---

7. [1974] ECR 1063.
8. [1991] ECR I-3187.
9. [1994] ECR I-2885.
10. [1978] ECR 1019.

breached the general principle of the protection of legitimate expectation, one of the general principles of Community law most frequently invoked before the Court. The Court held that a submission based on a breach of that principle was admissible in the context of an application under Article 173, since that principle formed part of the Community legal order, with the result that any failure to comply with it is 'an infringement of the Treaty or of any rule of law relating to its application' within the meaning of that provision. The rationale would appear to be that a legal principle, even though derived from national sources, which is accepted as a principle of Community law, is deemed to fall within the system established by the Treaty. *A fortiori*, this is the case where the general principle is one expressly recognised in the Treaty, such as the principle of non-discrimination set out in Articles 6 (formerly 7) and 40(2) of the EC Treaty.[11]

However, the fact that a general principle has been breached does not give an absolute entitlement to obtain the annulment of the measure at issue, as has been discussed in the context of principles of good administration. Another principle has long been established, which may be traced back to national sources, which means that breach of, for example, a general principle, will only lead to annulment where the applicant can show that the outcome would have been different if the principle had not been breached. The problem arose in a rather different context in Case 90/74 *De-boeck v Commission*,[12] a staff case. The action was for the annulment of an internal competition for the recruitment of secretarial assistants, and one submission of the applicant was that the notice of competition had not been preceded by a notice of vacancy as required by the Staff Regulations. The Court held that she had no interest to raise the point, since she was not eligible for transfer or promotion (the procedures which may precede the holding of a competition) without taking part in the competition, and she had in fact taken part in the competition. This followed an Opinion delivered by A.G. Warner in which he briefly reviewed the situation in the Member States, contrasting the tradition in French law and French derived systems whereby a person having an interest in the result[13] may raise any ground for the annulment of the act in

11. Case C-309/89 *Codorniu v Council* [1994] ECR I-1853.
12. [1975] ECR 1123.
13. Conseil d'Etat, 17 January 1947, p. 668.

question, with the view, *inter alios*, of Lord Wilberforce in *Malloch v Aberdeen Corporation*[14] that a 'breach of procedure, whether called a failure of natural justice, or an essential administrative fault, cannot give (the appellant) a remedy in the courts, unless behind it there is something of substance which has been lost by the failure' – and decisions by the Danish, Dutch and German courts that a plaintiff cannot complain of irregularities which have not caused him any harm.

What is interesting in this matter is not so much the result of the comparative study as the fact that the Court had previously reached the same conclusion despite the French view having been forcefully put. This illustrates both the difficulty of being able to make a definite pronouncement as to the origin of general principles applied by the Court – the judges cannot really be separated from their legal heritage, even if no specific mention is made of comparative analyses – and the danger of regarding Community law as an extension of French administrative law. The problem arose clearly in Case 37/72 *Marcato v Commission*,[15] with regard to the omission of an age limit in a notice of competition. A.G. Mayras put forward the classical French view: 'A candidate not admitted to a competition has an incontestable interest in challenging the working of the competition from which he considers himself to have been illegally excluded. He cannot be held to be precluded from pleading a point of law, whatever it may be.'

The Court, however, did not apply this rule, and looked instead to the interest of the applicant in having an age-limit fixed, noting that the setting of an age-limit could only have resulted in eliminating the applicant himself from the competition.

Examples may also be found in competition proceedings, as in Joined Cases 209-215 and 218/78 *Van Landewyck v Commission*.[16] It was there claimed that the Commission had wrongly communicated certain confidential information to the complainants, but the Court held that this could not lead to the annulment of the decision unless it could be shown that the decision would have been different in the absence of that irregularity; it was in fact found that the information had not enabled the complainant to put forward any argument likely to affect the substance of the decision.

14. [1971] 1 WLR at p. 1595.
15. [1973] ECR 361.
16. [1980] ECR 3125 at p. 3239.

This rule also applies in actions brought by Member States (and presumably EC institutions): in Case 259/85 *France v Commission*,[17] it was held, in the context of State aids, that even a Member State must show that the decision at issue would have had a different outcome if the alleged procedural breach had not occurred.

Plea of illegality

Since Article 184 of the EC Treaty refers expressly to the grounds for annulment set out in Article 173 of the EC Treaty, the same considerations would appear to apply here. What, however, may be noted in the context of the present book is that the Court has developed the plea of illegality into a general principle that an individual who is permitted to challenge an act which is individual in nature may at the same time contest the legality of the general legislation on which the individual act is based and which he is not permitted to challenge directly. Although Article 36 of the ECSC Treaty only envisages that the illegality of the underlying general decision may be invoked where the applicant is seeking the annulment of a decision imposing a pecuniary sanction or periodic penalty payment, this was held in Case 9/56 *Meroni v HA*[18] to be merely a specific application of a general principle recognised also in the EC and Euratom Treaties allowing the applicant to question the legality of the general decisions and recommendation on which any individual decision is based. Article 184 of the EC Treaty and Article 156 of the Euratom Treaty allow the 'inapplicability' of a Regulation to be invoked in proceeding in which it is at issue, but in Case 92/78 *Simmenthal v Commission*[19] it was held that the scope of Article 184 of the EC Treaty should extend to acts of the Community institutions which, even if not in the form of a Regulation, nonetheless produce analogous effects, and hence could not be challenged directly by anyone other than a Community institution or a Member State; in that case, the applicant was able to plead the illegality of general notices of invitation to tender on which the decision at issue was based.[20]

---

17. [1987] ECR 4393.
18. [1957 and 1958] ECR 133.
19 [1979] ECR 777.
20. See also Cases 181-184/86 *Del Plato v Commission* [1987] ECR 4991, where Commission methods of procedure were held to constitute a general act susceptible to the plea of illegality.

References from national courts

Article 177 of the EC Treaty and the parallel provisions of the other Treaties are not specific as to the grounds on which the Court may declare Community legislation invalid on a reference for a preliminary ruling from a national court. The result, therefore, is that there are numerous cases in which, on a reference from a national court, the European Court has held a Community measure invalid simply because, for example, it breaches the principle of non-discrimination,[21] or breaches the principle of proportionality,[22] or breaches the principle of the protection of legitimate expectations.[23] Furthermore, questions of *locus standi* and whether or not a litigant has an interest in the alleged breach of a general principle are essentially for the national court to determine, subject to the caveat discussed in Chapter 4 that a litigant who clearly could have brought a direct action for annulment but failed to do so in time cannot raise a question of the validity of the Community act at issue.[24]

Liability in damages

Mention has already been made[25] of the fact that the EC Treaty refers in its Article 215 to non-contractual liability in damages as being imposed 'in accordance with the general principles common to the laws of the Member States', which is the only express mention of general principles derived from the laws of the Member States in the Treaties. Before turning to the question of the extent to which breach of general principles may give rise to liability in damages, it may be observed that the Community law in this area has therefore been influenced by national principles not only with regard to the basis of liability, but also with regard to such matters as the development of a concept of contributory negligence giving rise to a reduction in the damages payable, but not necessarily

---

21. Cases 103 and 145/77 *Royal Scholten Honig v Intervention Board* [1978] ECR 2037.
22. Case 18/84 *ED and F. Mann v Intervention Board* [1985] ECR 2889.
23. Case 120/86 *Mulder* [1988] ECR 2321.
24. Case C-188/92 *TWD Textilwerke Deggendorf v Bundesminister für Wirtschaft* [1994] ECR I-833.
25. See Chapter 1.

their elimination,[26] and in discussion of the question whether there may be 'no-fault' liability under Articles 178 and 215 of the EC Treaty, where express reference was made the German concept of 'Sonderopfer' (special sacrifice) and the French concept of 'rupture de l'égalité devant les charges publiques' (unequal discharge of public burdens).[27]

With regard to liability for harm caused by binding normative acts, it has consistently been held since Case 5/71 *Schöppenstedt v Council*[28] that 'where legislative action involving measures of economic policy is concerned, the Community does not incur non-contractual liability for damage suffered by individuals as a consequence of that action ... unless a sufficiently flagrant violation of a superior rule of law for the protection of the individual has occurred', with the substitution of the word 'serious' for 'flagrant' in more recent judgments. It will be seen that rules derived from the Treaty itself and the general principles of Community law recognised by the Court may constitute such 'superior rules'.[29] Conceptually, the recognition of 'superior rules' indicates clearly that in the context of the European Community there are certain fundamental rules of law which can never be overcome by the Community institutions, whatever form of words they may choose to use; in other words, the fundamental general principles of Community law such as non-discrimination, the protection of legitimate expectation, and the principle of proportionality have a higher legal status than any secondary Community legislation.

However, the fact that a superior rule has been breached may nevertheless not in itself be sufficiently 'serious' to give rise to liability in damages, as appears from Joined Cases 83 and 94/76, etc., *Bayerische HNL v Council and Commission*.[30] The act there at issue was a Regulation effectively requiring manufacturers of animal feeding-stuffs to purchase intervention skimmed-milk powder, which was held to breach both the specific principle of non-discrimination enounced in Article 40(2) of the EC Treaty and the general principle of proportionality. Nevertheless, the Court stated that 'individuals may be required ... to accept within reasonable

---

26. See e.g. Case C-308/87 *Grifoni v Euratom* [1990] ECR I-1203 and Case 145/83 *Adams v Commission* [1985] ECR 3539.
27. Case 59/83 *Biovilac* [1984] ECR 4057.
28. [1971] ECR 975.
29. See pp. 130–2 below.
30. [1978] ECR 1209, 1224–1225.

limits certain harmful effects on their economic interests as a result of a legislative measure without being able to obtain compensation form public funds even if that measure has been declared null and void', and it was held that, since the Regulation increased production costs only by a little more than 2 per cent, which was considerably smaller that the variations in the world market prices of similar feeding-stuffs, 'the effects of the Regulation on the profit-earning capacity of the undertakings did not ultimately exceed the bounds of the economic risks inherent in the activities of the agricultural sectors concerned'.

By way of contrast, in Case 238/78 *Ireks-Arkady v Council and Commission*,[31] where the Regulation at issue had been held to breach the general principle of equality of treatment in so far as it abolished production refunds on quellmehl whilst retaining them for pre-gelatinised starch, it was found that the damage alleged to have been caused 'goes beyond the bounds of the economic risks inherent in the activities of the sector concerned', although emphasis was also laid on the fact that a limited number of producers were affected and that the termination of the refunds in question ended an equality of treatment with producers of maize starch which had existed since the beginning of the common organisation of the market in cereals (in 1962). In essence, however, it might be concluded that a breach of a superior rule will be regarded as sufficiently 'serious' if the harm caused goes beyond the Court's assessment of the inherent economic risks of the sector concerned, although in those cases the Court also emphasised that the Community would not incur liability unless the institution concerned manifestly and gravely disregarded the limits on the exercise of its powers, a criterion which takes account of the conduct of the institution rather than the severity of the harm caused, and which seems difficult to reconcile with the possible acceptance of no-fault liability in this area.

An example of the dividing line between conduct which will and will not give rise to liability may be found in Cases C-104/89 and C-37/90 *Mulder v Council and Commission*.[32] These were actions brought by dairy producers who had agreed to give up dairy production for a period of five years under an earlier Community scheme and had not produced any milk during the year (1983 in

---

31. [1979] ECR 2955, 2973.
32. [1992] ECR I-3061.

their case) taken as the base year for calculating the milk-quotas, and had therefore not been granted any milk-quota when the quota system was introduced in 1984 by Council Regulation 857/84. However, following judgments of the Court holding this legislation unlawful,[33] they had subsequently been granted a quota based on 60 per cent of their production during the year before they began to take part in the 'outgoers' scheme by Council Regulation 764/89, and this also was held to be unlawful by the Court.[34] In both instances, the legislation was held to breach the general principle of the protection of legitimate expectations, but in the action for damages it was held that only the initial legislation granting no quota at all gave rise to liability on the part of the Community institutions.

The explanation given by the Court is that, in taking no account at all of the situation of the producers concerned, the Community institutions had manifestly and gravely disregarded the limits on the exercise of their powers, and this failure fell outside the normal inherent economic risks of the sector concerned. On the other hand, the legislation which gave the outgoers a quota based on 60 per cent of their previous production did take account of their situation (even if it breached the principle of the protection of legitimate expectations), and it represented a choice of economic policy which reflected the need not to upset the fragile balance achieved on the milk market and the need to balance the interests of the outgoers with those of other producers. In the Court's view, the Council had thus taken account of a higher public interest and had not manifestly and gravely disregarded the limits on the exercise of its powers.

It may be submitted that, in determining whether a breach of a superior rule is sufficiently serious, this judgment places rather more emphasis on the institution's conduct than on the severity of the harm suffered by the applicant; it may respectfully be doubted whether a loss of 40 per cent of production is a normal trading risk.

Be that as it may, liability for the harm caused by legislative acts may extend not only to a breach of a superior rule arising from the substance of the act, but also from, for example, the circumstances

---

33. Case 120/86 *Mulder* [1988] ECR 2321, Case 170/86 *Deetzen* [1988] ECR 2355.

34. Case C-189/89 *Spagl* [1990] ECR I-4539; Case C-217/89 *Pastätter* [1990] ECR I-4585.

surrounding its introduction. This was established in Case 74/74 *CNTA v Commission*,[35] where it was held that to abolish certain monetary compensatory amounts without allowing any transitional measures in the absence of overriding considerations of public interest breached the applicant's legitimate expectations. The facts arose at a time when monetary compensatory amounts were calculated in terms of the dollar, and the Court took the view that 'a trader may legitimately expect that for transactions irrevocably undertaken by him ... no unforeseeable alteration will occur which could have the effect of causing him inevitable loss, by re-exposing him to the exchange risk'. While it may be that a reasonable trader could regard the original monetary compensatory amounts based on the values of national currencies in terms of the dollar as covering the exchange risk, it may be doubted whether he or she could so regard the later form of monetary compensatory amounts, which, until they were abolished at the end of 1992, covered the difference between a 'representative rate' for a national currency determined by the Council and the current value of that currency in terms of a basket of Community currencies.

Constraints on the activities of Member States

General considerations

General principles of Community law govern the activities of Member States to the extent that, but only to the extent that, they are acting within the scope of Community law. Thus, while the principle of equal treatment of men and women could be applied directly to the activities of Community institutions,[36] it could only be applied to national authorities within the scope of specific Community legislation.[37] Similarly, while national safeguard measures taken in relation to the free movement of goods under Article 36 of the EC Treaty are subject to a proportionality test,[38] national restrictions on capital movements at a time when the Community legislation did not require those movements to be liberalised were

---

35. [1975] ECR 533.
36. Cases 75 and 117/82 *Razzouk and Beydouin v Commission* [1984] ECR 1509.
37. Case C-147/95 *Dimosia Epicheirisi Ilectrismou (DEI) v Evthimios Evrenopoulos* (17 April 1997).
38. Case 124/81 *Commission v United Kingdom* [1983] ECR 203.

not subject to such a test:[39] since such restrictions were a purely a matter of national law, there was no need to comply with principles of Community law such as proportionality or non-discrimination.

However, within the scope of Community law, general principles may give rise to both positive and negative obligations. By way of example, the principle of Community preference may require Member States to impose certain charges on goods imported from third countries which breach the effective uniformity of the Common Customs Tariff.[40] Indeed, it has been seen that to the extent Community law treats them as competent authorities, the actions of national authorities may be regarded as giving rise to legitimate expectations under Community law.[41]

Scope of the constraints

National authorities may, in particular, be regarded as acting within the scope of Community law where they are implementing a Community policy such as the Common Agricultural Policy, where they are acting under other express Community legislation, and where Community law itself permits them to impose certain restrictions on activities otherwise permitted or required to be permitted under Community law, notably in relation to the exercise of rights of free movement given under Community law.

In the context of the Common Agricultural Policy, although, at first sight, Article 40(3) prohibiting discrimination between producers, and the underlying general principle of non-discrimination, may seem only to govern the validity of Community legislation, the European Court held, as has been seen in Cases 201 and 202/85 *Klensch v Luxembourg Secretary of State for Agriculture*,[42] that it applies to any measure taken in the context of a common organisation of an agricultural market, whether that measure is taken by the Community authorities or the national authorities. Hence, in that case, the exercise by the Luxembourg government of its discretion under the milk-quota system to choose the reference year from which quotas would be calculated was held to be subject to the principle of non-discrimination.

[39.] Case 203/80 *Casati* [1981] ECR 2595.
[40.] See Chapter 2, pp. 15 and 16 above.
[41.] Cases C-153 and 204/94 *R v Commissioners of Customs and Excise, ex p Faroe Seafood* [1996] ECR I-2465.
[42.] [1986] ECR 3477.

It may also be observed that, within the scope of the Common Agricultural Policy, indeed again within the scope of the milk-quota rules, it has been held that Member States are bound by the general principle of Community law requiring respect for property rights.[43]

So far as actions by Member States governed by Community legislation are concerned, an example may be found in Case 222/84 *Johnston v Chief Constable of the RUC*.[44] Mrs. Johnston was faced with a certificate issued by the Secretary of State under the Northern Ireland Sex Discrimination Order stating that this certificate was 'conclusive evidence' that the conditions for derogating from the principle of equal treatment were fulfilled. In that context, the Court held that a provision of an EC directive, which required Member States to enable all persons who consider themselves wronged by sex discrimination to be able to pursue their claims by judicial process, was a reflection of a general principle of law underlying the constitutional traditions common to the Member States, and underlying also specific provisions of the Human Rights Convention. As noted in Chapter 5 above, the Court concluded that this general principle of effective judicial control meant that a certificate which claimed to be conclusive could not allow the competent authority to deprive an individual of the possibility of asserting by judicial process the rights conferred by the Directive.

An illustration of general principles constraining the powers of Member States where Community law itself enables them to impose certain restrictions on activities otherwise permitted or required to be permitted under Community law may be found in the first judgment of the European Court to refer specifically to particular provisions of the Convention on Human Rights.[45] This arose from an attempt by the French authorities to restrict the rights of residence of an Italian worker, who had taken rather too lively an interest in French domestic politics during the 'events' of 1968, by invoking grounds of public policy under Article 48 of the EC Treaty. The Court there stated that the limitations placed on the powers of Member States to control the movements of the citizens of other Member States under Community law were sim-

---

[43]. Case 5/88 *Wachauf v Bundesamt für Ernährung und Fortwirtschaft* [1989] ECR 2609.

[44]. [1986] ECR 1651.

[45]. Case 36/75 *Rutili v Ministre de l' Intérieur* [1975] ECR 1219.

ply a specific manifestation of a more general principle enshrined in various provisions of the Human Rights Convention providing that 'no restrictions in the interests of national security or public safety shall be placed on the rights secured by those articles other than such as are necessary for the protection of those interests in a democratic society'. The necessary implication of the judgment was that to restrict a migrant worker's rights of residence because of his trade union activities was not something necessary for the protection of national security or public safety in a democratic society.

In this context, the principle of proportionality is of particular importance, as has been seen in relation to national restrictions on the free movement of goods.[46] It may indeed be suggested that the Court applies a relatively strict test of proportionality to national provisions which operate within the sphere of the limited derogations provided for by the EC Treaty in relation to the operation of the fundamental Four Freedoms. Thus, for example, in Case 118/75 *Watson and Belmann*,[47] it was held that while Italy could require foreign nationals to notify their presence, it was not justified in imposing a penalty so disproportionate that it became an obstacle to the free movement of persons.

Furthermore, the same approach has subsequently been followed with regard to national measures which at first sight would appear to sanction a failure to comply with a requirement of Community law but which might indirectly affect the exercise of Community law rights, as may be illustrated in relation to Council Directive 80/1263, which provided a mechanism under which a holder of a driving licence issued in one Member State who took up permanent residence in another Member State could exchange the licence for one issued by the host State. However, it provided for the original licence to be recognised in the host State only for a period of one year, which meant that the exchange had to take place in that period – a requirement which was eliminated by the entry into force in 1996 of Council Directive 91/439 providing for mutual recognition of driving licences. In Case C-193/94 *Skanavi and Chryssanthakopoulos*,[48] Mrs. Skanavi and her husband took up residence in Germany in 1992 in order to take over a German

46. See Chapter 3 above.
47. [1976] ECR 1185.
48. [1996] ECR I-929.

company. Mrs. Skanavi was stopped by police in Germany just over a year later while still using her Greek licence, and was charged under the relevant German regulation for driving without a driving licence, an offence punishable by up to one year's imprisonment.

The European Court considered that at the relevant time, the requirement to exchange driving licence imposed by Member States was valid under Article 52 of the EC Treaty in the absence of complete harmonisation. However, it also noted that, although under Directive 80/1263 a licence had to be exchanged within one year, the licence remained valid in the State which issued it after that period. Hence, the issue of a driving licence in the host State did not constitute the basis of the right to drive a motor vehicle in the that State's territory, and the obligation to exchange driving licences was essentially a way of meeting administrative requirements. While acknowledging that in the absence of Community rules the Member States remained competent to impose penalties for breach of such an obligation, the Court (following A.G. Léger) pointed out that in laying down such formalities they were not entitled to impose penalties so disproportionate to the gravity of the infringement that it became an obstacle to the free movement of persons; that would be especially so if the penalty consisted of imprisonment. Furthermore, the Court considered that such exposure to criminal penalties, even where they were financial in nature, would be disproportionate to the gravity of the infringement in view of the likely consequences of a criminal conviction, e.g. in relation to the exercise of a trade or profession by an employed or self-employed person, particularly with regard to access to certain activities or certain offices, which would constitute a further, lasting restriction on freedom of movement.

On a more substantive issue, the principle of proportionality has also been used to test the legitimacy of certain public sector employment policies in Member States. In Cases C-259/91, C-331/91 and C-332/91 *Allué v Università degli Studi di Venezia*,[49] the question arose as to the compatibility with Article 48(2) of the EC Treaty on free movement of workers of Italian legislation limiting the duration of contracts of employment for foreign language assistants at a university to one year, where that provision essentially concerned workers who were nationals of other Member

49. [1993] ECR I-4309.

States. It was held that such provisions could be compatible with the terms of Article 48(2), but only to the extent that they respected the principle of proportionality, that is to say, constituted appropriate and necessary measures to achieve the desired aim. Thus, Community law did not preclude a Member State from concluding with foreign language assistants contracts of employment for a specified period where, at the time of appointment, it appeared that the teaching requirements did not extend beyond such a period. On the other hand, contracts which were intended to meet continuing educational needs, as with languages whose study was compulsory or which were known to be in great demand, had to be concluded for an indeterminate period in the same way as the employment relationships of other teachers meeting such needs. In the circumstances, the general restriction to one year of the duration of the contracts with the possibility of renewal constituted for assistants an insecurity factor with regard to the maintenance of the employment relationship and was likely to allow abuse by the national administration. This was therefore contrary to Article 48(2) of the EC Treaty.

In more general terms, as the Court put it in the context of provision of services under Article 59 of the EC Treaty in Case C-288/89 *Gouda*,[50] the application of national provisions to providers of services established in other Member States must be such as to guarantee the achievement of the intended aim and must not go beyond that which is necessary in order to achieve that objective. In other words, it must not be possible to obtain the same result by less restrictive means.

---

50. [1991] ECR I-4007 at para. 15.

CHAPTER NINE

Influence of principles of Community law within the legal systems of the United Kingdom

The issues

It is clear that general principles of Community law are applicable at the national level in a Community law context. However, the more general question remains as to the extent to which legal techniques, concepts, and principles developed in the context of European Community law, in particular by the European Court of Justice, have had an effect within the legal systems of the United Kingdom. There has been an obvious influence where national remedies have had to be developed to deal with breaches of Community law, and with hindsight it can be seen that courts in the United Kingdom have anticipated the approach of the European Court in some instances.

An example occurred when the question as to whether there might be a liability in damages for harm caused by ministerial acts in breach of EC law eventually arose before the English courts in an action brought by French poultry producers against the Ministry of Agriculture,[1] following the judgment of the European Court holding that United Kingdom restrictions on the import of poultry meat from France were in fact a breach of Article 30 of the EEC Treaty and were not justified on health grounds.[2] In the Court of Appeal in that action for damages, Parker LJ, who delivered the majority judgment, invoked the case-law of the European Court on the liability of the Community institutions to pay damages for harm caused by legislation under Article 215 as a justification for limiting the circumstances under which such liability might occur

---

[1.] *Bourgoin v MAFF* [1985] 3 All ER 585.
[2.] Case 40/82 *Commission v UK* [1982] ECR 2793.

when Community law was breached by a United Kingdom Minister. While the merits of the analogy have been doubted,[3] it was an illustration of a general principle of Community law derived from the laws of the original Member States being received back into the national legal system of a Member State which joined in the second wave. In the result, the Ministry of Agriculture settled the case by paying the French producers £3.5 million.[4] However, a decade later, the European Court took the same approach in Cases C-46/93 *Brasserie du Pêcheur* and C-48/93 *Factortame III*.[5] With regard to the conditions under which a Member State could incur such liability, the Court accepted that they must in principle be the same as those governing the liability of Community institutions under Article 215 of the EC Treaty, taking account in particular of the margin of discretion left to the author of the act at issue. However, while under Article 215 a Community institution which enjoys a wide discretion does not incur liability unless it manifestly and gravely disregards the limits on the exercise of its powers, the Court pointed out that Member States do not systematically have a wide discretion when acting in fields governed by Community law. The Court nevertheless held that in the two cases at issue the Member States did enjoy a wide discretion and indicated the criteria governing liability in such circumstances: the provision breached must be intended to confer rights on individuals; the breach must be sufficiently serious; and there must be a direct causal link between the breach of the obligation on the State and the damage sustained by the injured parties.

With regard to the seriousness of the breach, the Court suggested that account should be taken of the clarity and precision of the rule breached, the discretion it left to national or Community authorities, whether or not the infringement and the harm caused was intentional, whether or not any error of law was excusable, whether a position taken by a Community institution had contributed to the breach, and whether national measures or practices contrary to Community law had been adopted or retained. In particular, the Court emphasised that a breach of Community law will be sufficiently serious if it persists despite a judgment finding that there is an infringement, or where there is a preliminary ruling

---

[3.] See e.g. Temple Lang, *The Duties of National Courts under the Constitutional Law of the European Community* (Exeter, 1987).

[4.] Hansard 23 July 1986, Vol.102, No.156, Col. 116.

[5.] [1996] ECR I-1029.

or settled case-law making it clear that the conduct in question does constitute an infringement; in *Factortame III* it also suggested that account might be taken of the views expressed by the Commission at the relevant time. On the other hand, the Court held that there was no requirement to show fault (a concept which in the Court's view had different meanings in different legal systems) on the part of the national authorities other than a sufficiently serious breach of Community law.

The aim of this chapter is, however, not only to see what influence general principles of Community law may have had where United Kingdom authorities are administering Community law, but also to see what, if any, influence they may have had in situations in no way directly governed by Community law. For this purpose, reference may be made to three concepts or principles commonly used by the European Court of Justice: purposive interpretation, the principle of the protection of legitimate expectations, and the principle of proportionality.

It is, of course, difficult if not impossible to show that certain principles have been developed within the legal systems of the United Kingdom solely because they exist as general principles of Community law. Nevertheless, it may be argued that there has been a remarkable degree of parallelism between English law in particular, and Community law, with regard to the development of certain principles since the accession of the United Kingdom to the European Communities.

Purposive interpretation

A particularly notable example concerns not a substantive general principle of Community law but one of its most widely used techniques, that of purposive or teleological interpretation. This principle has, of course, been of fundamental importance in giving effect to many of the basic provisions of the EC Treaty. Its development was also encouraged, however, by the fact that the text of any Community legislation is equally authentic in all the official languages of the Community, currently 11. Hence, there are many judgments where passages such as the following, taken from a decision given in 1973,[6] may be found:

6. Case 61/72 *Mij. PPW International v Hoofdproduktschap voor Akkerbouw-produkten* [1973] ECR 301.

No argument can be drawn either from any linguistic divergences between the various language versions, or from the multiplicity of the verbs used in one or other of those versions, as the meaning of the provisions in question must be determined with respect to their objective.

In the United Kingdom, on the other hand, while such an approach was not totally unknown, the tradition was to base interpretation very much upon linguistic analysis of the words used, and there was therefore a temptation to use this technique in the context of Community law. This may be seen in *R v Henn and Darby*,[7] where the question arose whether the United Kingdom prohibition on the importation of obscene articles constituted a measure equivalent to a quantitative restriction on imports from another Member State prohibited under Article 30 of the EC Treaty, the widest ranging provision of that Treaty with regard to the free movement of goods. The then Lord Chief Justice, Lord Widgery, suggested that where there was a *total* prohibition this could not be a 'quantitative' restriction, because there was no restriction by reference to a quantity. It does not take much imagination to envisage the extent to which there would be a single internal market if Member States really were actually free to impose total prohibitions on the entry of goods from other Member States. Article 30 has in fact been interpreted by the European Court as prohibiting 'rules enacted by Member States which are capable of hindering directly or indirectly, actually or potentially, intra-Community trade'. Fortunately, the House of Lords showed a greater awareness of the case-law of the European Court, and referred the matter to that Court for a preliminary ruling.[8] The European Court, held that the prohibition was indeed a measure equivalent to a quantitative restriction, but that it could be justified under Article 36 of the EC Treaty on grounds of public morality.

However, when the attempt was made a few years after Accession by Lord Denning in the Court of Appeal to use the European Court's technique in a context which did not involve Community law,[9] a technique which he described as being called in English by 'strange' words, 'the schematic and teleological' method of inter-

---

[7.] Case 34/79 *R v Henn and Darby* [1979] ECR 3795.
[8.] Ibid.
[9.] *Buchanan v Babco* [1977] 1 All ER 518.

pretation, but which he described with approval as involving the resolution of problems by looking at the design and purpose of the legislation, a rather different view was taken in the House of Lords. There Lord Wilberforce said,[10] in as many words, that he did not get assistance from methods *said* to be used in interpreting the EC Treaty by the Court of Justice of the European Communities.

By the mid-1980s, however, English judges dealing even with matters of 'lawyers' law' could be found expressly making use of purposive interpretation and calling it by that name. So, in *Bank of Scotland v Grimes*,[11] the judges of the Court of Appeal expressly stated that they were giving a purposive interpretation to section 8 of the Administration of Justice Act 1973, in order to be able to give relief from loss of possession of his house to a householder unable to pay off outstanding arrears under his mortgage, not only where the mortgage was of the traditional instalment type (which fell clearly within the provision), but also where it was of the endowment type (which did not fall so easily within the express words of the section).

A similar approach has also been taken in the House of Lords. In *Smalley v Crown Court, Warwick*[12] Lord Bridge looked at the purpose of sections 28 and 29 of the Supreme Court Act 1981. This excluded from judicial review a decision of the Crown Court relating to trial on indictment, and it no doubt excluded such a decision from judicial review because the Criminal Appeal Act 1968 provided a special system of criminal appeals. However, in this case he was concerned with an order of the Crown Court estreating the recognisance of a surety for a defendant who failed to surrender to his bail at the Crown Court. Unfortunately, the system of appeals laid down by the Criminal Appeal Act was only available to the person who had been tried on indictment. Therefore, the surety – that is the person who put up the financial guarantee that the defendant would appear – sought judicial review of the order. Although the order was in a literal sense a decision relating to trial on indictment, Lord Bridge said that he could discern no intelligible legislative purpose why the exclusion from judicial review of matters relating to trial on indictment should apply to such

10. [1977] 3 All ER 1048 at p. 1053.
11. [1985] 2 All ER 254.
12. [1985] 1 All ER 769 at p. 779.

an order, since the order could not affect the conduct of the trial and there was no sensible reason why an aggrieved surety should not have a remedy by way of judicial review.

More importantly, it may be argued that it was precisely because of the adoption of the purposive technique of interpretation that the House of Lords finally decided in *Pepper v Hart*[13] that reference could be made to Parliamentary material (i.e. in particular, Hansard) as an aid to the construction of legislation which is ambiguous or obscure or the literal meaning of which leads to an absurdity, where the Parliamentary material clearly discloses the mischief aimed at or the legislative intention lying behind the ambiguous or obscure words. In his speech, with which the majority concurred, Lord Browne-Wilkinson indicated[14] that he accepted the submissions of counsel (Lord Lester QC) which took as their starting point the fact that the courts were adopting a purposive approach to interpretation, seeking to discover the parliamentary intention behind the words used.

There does, however, appear to be a limit, in that the English courts have been unwilling to adopt a purposive interpretation where it would prevent an individual deriving a benefit to which he would be entitled on a literal interpretation. This appears from the action brought against the Broadcasting Complaints Commission by Dr. David Owen,[15] which incidentally contains one of the clearest statements of the acceptance of the principle of purposive interpretation, when May LJ said: 'On modern principles of construction it is clearly legitimate to adopt a purposive approach and to hold that a statutory provision does apply to a given situation when it was clearly intended to do so even though it may not so apply on a strict literal interpretation.' However, he added that he did not think that the converse was true and that it was not legitimate to adopt a purposive construction so as to preclude the application of a statute to a situation to which on its purely literal construction it would apply.

By way of contrast, it has to be admitted that the European Court of Justice has been quite prepared to apply purposive interpretation against the individual who might have expected to rely on the literal interpretation of Community legislation. This is illus-

---

13. [1993] 1 All ER 42.
14. [1993] 1 All ER 42 at p. 64.
15. *R v Broadcasting Complaints Commission ex p Owen* [1985] 2 All ER 522.

trated by the stories of the unfortunate Messrs. Padovani[16] and von Menges.[17] Mr. Padovani tried to take advantage of an EC Regulation which provided for a reduction in the level of import levies charged on imports of cereals when such cereals were imported by sea into Italy. The boat containing his cereals arrived at an Italian port and all the customs formalities relating to the importation of the cereals were carried out in that Italian port, so that the goods were technically imported into Italy. However, the boat did not unload in the Italian port; instead it sailed round to the Netherlands. It was held by the Court that although Mr. Padovani's importation might have fallen within the literal words of the regulation, nevertheless the reduction in levy for cereals imported by sea into Italy was intended to take account of the high port and unloading costs incurred in Italy, and was therefore only available if the cereals were not only technically imported, but also actually unloaded in Italy.

Mr. von Menges, on the other hand, took advantage of legislation designed to encourage farmers to leave dairy production. He did indeed get rid of his herd of dairy cows as required under the Regulation, but he replaced them with a flock of sheep, which he used not for producing meat or wool but for producing sheep's milk. Whilst sheep's milk did not technically fall within the common organisation of the market in milk, the Court nevertheless held that it competed with products falling within that organisation, so that his new activity was not helping to reduce the surplus of dairy production, which was the aim of the scheme, and therefore he could not take advantage of the subsidies available under the dairy conversion scheme.

Legitimate expectations

The principle of the protection of legitimate expectation, to turn to one of the major general principles of European Community Law, is, as has been noted in Chapter 4, generally regarded as having been inspired by the German principle of 'Vertrauensschutz', a principle held by the German courts to underlie certain provisions of the German Basic Law. In the form developed by the European Court of Justice, as has been seen, while expectations may not be

16. Case 69/84 *Padovani* [1985] ECR 1859.
17. Case 109/84 *von Menges* [1985] ECR 1289.

protected *contra legem*, an expectation may nevertheless prevail even against an act which constitutes general binding legislation in certain circumstances. Perhaps the classic example is to be found in the judgment given in Case 81/72 *Commission v Council*[18] in the context of a dispute between the Commission and the Council as to the calculation of annual increases in the salaries of officials of the European Communities.

It will be recalled[19] that in the result, the Court held that a Council Regulation was invalid as contravening the policy laid down by an earlier informal Council Decision. In so deciding, the Court did not follow the Opinion of A.G. Warner, who cited case-law in the Member States, and in particular England and France, to suggest that there was no such principle. Indeed, it may be suggested that the traditional English attitude that the Crown, that is central government, could not fetter its future executive action was best shown in a case which arose from the First World War.[20] It would appear that the Swedish owners of a ship were induced to send it to a British port by a letter from the British legation in Stockholm stating that it would be released if it sailed to the United Kingdom with a cargo of approved goods. Having arrived in a British port with these goods, the ship was then refused clearance; the owners sued for damages, but it was held that the government could not hamper its freedom of action in matters which concerned the welfare of the State. Such a principle had also been applied to the activities of local authorities and public corporations. There were, however, exceptions. In 1972, just before the United Kingdom's accession, legitimate expectations (which it must be said, was a phrase introduced into English law by Lord Denning as early as 1969),[21] were enforced by the English Court of Appeal against a local government authority, if not a central government authority, in a case involving Liverpool Corporation and the licensing of taxis.[22] Under powers given by the Town Police Clauses Act of 1847 to license such a number of hackney coaches or carriages as they think fit in their area, Liverpool Corporation had since 1948 limited the number of taxis to 300. At a Council

---

18. [1973] ECR 575 at p. 584. See Chapter 4 above.
19. See Chapter 4, p. 55 above.
20. *Rederiaktiebolaget Amphitrite* [1921] 3 QB 500.
21. *Schmidt v Secretary of State for Home Affairs* [1969] 1 All ER 904.
22. *R v Liverpool Corporation, ex p Liverpool Taxi Fleet Operators' Association* [1972] 2 All ER 589.

meeting in August 1971, an undertaking was given that this number would not be increased until a private bill controlling private hire cars had been enacted. Nevertheless, in December 1971, the Council resolved to increase the number of licences for 1972. This was challenged by the Taxi Fleet Operators Association, and it was held by the Court of Appeal that although the Council must make up its own mind as to the policy it wished to follow, it must act fairly to all concerned, notably to present licensees and to would-be licensees. Hence, although it could depart from its undertaking, it must do so only after due and proper consideration of the representations of all those interested. In the result, an order was issued to the Corporation preventing it from acting on its resolution to increase the number of licences until it had heard representations on behalf of those interested, including the Taxi Fleet Operators Association.

Subsequently, however, the House of Lords has indicated that legitimate expectations may also be enforced against central government authorities, even against a Minister acting under powers derived from the royal prerogative, and in a context not totally dissimilar from that involved in the dispute between the EC Commission and Council which has just been mentioned. This occurred in the famous GCHQ dispute.[23] The Civil Service unions there sought judicial review of an instruction issued by the Minister of the Civil Service, that is the Prime Minister, that the terms and conditions of civil servants at GCHQ should be revised so as to exclude membership of any trade union other than a departmental staff association approved by the Director of GCHQ. The argument put on behalf of the unions was essentially that the employees of GCHQ had a legitimate expectation that there would be prior consultation before any important change was made in their conditions of service.

The legal basis of this claim was clearly analysed by Lord Fraser as being that even where a person claiming some benefit or privilege has no legal right to it, as a matter of private law, he may have a legitimate expectation of receiving the benefit or privilege, and, if so, the courts will protect his expectation by judicial review as a matter of public law. Indeed, he went so far as to say that legitimate expectations of the type at issue would always relate to a

---

23. *Council of Civil Service Unions v Minister for the Civil Service* [1984] 3 All ER 935.

benefit or privilege to which a claimant had no right in private law, and it might even be to one which conflicted with his private law rights, presumably the express terms of employment. The evidence was that since GCHQ began in 1947, prior consultation had been the invariable rule when conditions of service were to be significantly altered, and he concluded that if there had been no question of national security involved, the unions would have had a legitimate expectation that the Minister would consult them before issuing the instruction.

Leaving aside the obvious continental influence of the terminology of public law and private law which has become fashionable since 1982 in administrative law cases before the House of Lords, dare one suggest that here, just as in the European Court's judgment in *Commission v Council*, there is a recognition that expectations can be derived which can override the strict legal situation and which will be protected by the courts.

An illustration which did not involve questions of national security can be found in *Ex p Khan*.[24] It was there held that the recipient of a Home Office circular would have a legitimate expectation that the criteria and procedures laid down in that circular for the admission of a child into the United Kingdom for the purpose of her adoption would be followed, and the Secretary of State could only apply different criteria and procedures if he first gave the recipient of the circular a proper opportunity to make representations as to why such different criteria and procedures should not be followed in his case.

It may however be observed that all the English cases mentioned above involve the protection of expectations as to procedures to be followed, and the same would appear to be true in Scotland,[25] whereas in European Community law it is clear that substantive expectations may equally be protected, as in the *Mulder* case with regard to the allocation of milk-quota to those who had participated in the Community outgoers' scheme.[26] However, in the United Kingdom, it appears to be a matter of some controversy as to whether substantive legitimate expectations may be protected.[27]

24. [1985] 1 All ER 40.
25. *Lakin Ltd v Secretary of State for Scotland* 1988 SLT 780.
26. Case 120/86 *Mulder* [1988] ECR 2321; Case 170/86 *Deetzen* [1988] ECR 2355. See Chapter 4 above.
27. See Craig, 'Substantive Legitimate Expectations in Domestic and Community Law' (1996) CLJ 289.

Such a possibility has been denied outright,[28] but the concept was discussed in detail by Sedley J in *R v Ministry of Agriculture, ex p Hamble Fisheries.*[29] In the context of the grant of sea fishing licences, the Ministry of Agriculture, Fisheries and Food (MAFF) had developed a policy which promoted capacity aggregation by transfer of licences from two or more smaller vessels to a larger vessel, provided that the total capacity of the fleet was not increased. Early in 1992, the owners of a beam trawler, 'Nellie', had bought two vessels with a view to transferring their licences to the 'Nellie' in line with that policy, and in line with the capacity restrictions were proceeding to downsize the engines of the 'Nellie'. However, it was becoming apparent that existing restrictions on beam trawling were proving inadequate to protect the pressure stocks in the North Sea (i.e. stocks of fish that are not sustainable at current capacity levels of commercial fishing), and in March 1992 MAFF decided to reassess the licensing system for the area and introduced an immediate moratorium on the transfer and aggregation of pressure stock licences on to beam trawlers fishing in the North Sea or West of Scotland waters. In order to restrict the number of vessels eligible, MAFF provided that fishermen could not qualify for a licence unless they had a historic record of fishing in these areas. Hence, only existing operating vessels could apply for the new licences.

Pursuant to this policy MAFF had refused the 'Nellie' a licence as it did not qualify for a licence under either the new rules or under designated exceptions to those rules. The owners of 'Nellie' therefore made an application for judicial review of the MAFF decision refusing the applicants a North Sea beam trawler licence on the grounds that they had a legitimate expectation that any change in the licensing system would not frustrate the completion of the process of licence aggregation which had up until this point been promoted by MAFF, and that proper transitional provisions should have been included in the new policy to ensure that fishermen who had irrevocably entered into commitments on the basis of the previous policy were not disadvantaged as a result.

Although Sedley J found as a matter of English law that substantive as well as procedural legitimate expectations could be pro-

---

28. Laws J in *R v Secretary of State for Transport, ex p Richmond London Borough Council* [1994] 1 All ER 73.
29. [1995] 2 All ER 714.

tected, the case was argued almost entirely in terms of the jurisprudence of the European Court. Accepting the value of these submissions, Sedley J declared that, in the context of implementing the common agricultural policy of the European Community, if each Member State were governed in carrying out its part of this joint exercise by no jurisprudence other than its own domestic law, a major objective of the policy would be frustrated. He concluded that the availability of eventual recourse to the Court of Justice from and against all Member States in relation to the carrying out of the common agricultural policy must require domestic courts to have full regard to the jurisprudence of the Court of Justice. Reference was also expressly made to the definition and scope of the principle as discussed by Professor Schwarze in his book *European Administrative Law*.[30]

Sedley J rejected the argument that the principle was based on the principle of estoppel, pointing out that public authorities cannot be estopped from performing their public duties, and turned to the question of what makes an expectation legitimate. First, he distinguished between a promise and a practice, observing that in the former case it was relatively straightforward to decide whether the promisor should be held to it. However, in the case of practices, he observed that where the material practice was generated by policy which is itself liable to change, the practice could not logically be expected to survive a policy change. He went on to draw a distinction between expectations that are 'reasonable', but which might not be legitimate, and therefore not protected, and expectations which legitimately give rise to a right to the individual concerned and corresponding obligations.

With regard to policy changes, Sedley J noted that it might be thought that no expectation, however reasonable, can survive a change in policy. However, it was also well established that 'it is a misuse of power for a public body to act unfairly or unjustly towards the private citizen when there is no overriding public interest to warrant it'.[31] As Sedley J put it, 'it is the court's task to recognise the constitutional importance of ministerial freedom to formulate and to reformulate policy; but it is equally the court's duty to protect the interests of those individuals whose expectation

---

[30.] London, 1992.
[31.] Quoting Lord Denning MR in *HTV Ltd v Price Commission* [1976] ICR 170 at p. 185.

of different treatment has a legitimacy which in fairness outtops the policy choice which threatens to frustrate it'.

Applying this test to the case before him, Sedley J dismissed the application for judicial review. The Minister was in his view entitled to draw the line as tightly around the existing fleet as could fairly be done. He had considered the position of the fishermen who were incipiently dependent on North Sea beam trawling; but it was in his judgment not unfair, in the light of the government's legitimate policy imperatives and objectives, to exclude from the policy's transitional provisions enterprises in the position of the applicant, notwithstanding that the latter had embarked upon the acquisition of transferable licence entitlements in the anticipation, and the genuine intention, of being able in due course to aggregate them onto a vessel for the purposes of beam trawling.

However, when the question of legitimate expectations came before the Court of Appeal in *R v Secretary of State for the Home Department, ex p Hargreaves*,[32] Hirst LJ took the line that the earlier cases were concerned with matters of procedure, and acceded to the view that Sedley J's approach was 'heresy'. In his view, on matters of substance, the test was not that of legitimate expectation but that of '*Wednesbury*[33] reasonableness', which will be considered in the next section of this chapter. Heresy or not, it may be suggested that Sedley J could have gone further than he did in following the Community law principle of legitimate expectation: to the extent that MAFF was implementing the EC common fisheries policy, it may be argued that it was subject to the Community law principle as such.[34] Even as a matter of English law, however, it would appear that the matter is not closed. In his speech in the House of Lords in *Pierson v Secretary of State for the Home Department*,[35] Lord Steyn referred to the fact that counsel for the Home Office had argued that the doctrine of legitimate expectations merely gave protection against procedural unfairness, and stated: 'This is a controversial question. Counsel is not necessarily right.'

If it really is the case that the protection of legitimate expectations in English law is limited to procedural matters, then it is a

---

[32.] [1997] 1 All ER 397 at p. 412.

[33.] *Associated Provincial Picture Houses v Wednesbury Corporation* [1948] 1 KB 223.

[34.] See Chapter 8 above.

[35.] [1997] 3 All ER 577 at p. 606.

much narrower concept than the general principle of Community law – and perhaps reflects a judicial reluctance to be involved in adjudication of policy issues which has also limited the acceptance of the principle of proportionality, as will be seen. At the least, however, express discussion of the case-law of the European Court forms an element in the debate.

Before leaving the topic, however, it may be observed that in holding that the change of policy in *R v Ministry of Agriculture, ex p Hamble Fisheries*[36] did not breach legitimate expectations, Sedley J stated that 'the means adopted bore a fair proportion to the end in view, both in respect of what was included in, and of that which was excluded from, the [transitional] provisions'. In other words, it would appear that in his view, proportionality was a guiding factor in balancing the public interests underlying the change in policy in relation to the interests of those who had been acting in reliance of the previous policy – which leads to a consideration of the extent to which proportionality as such has been accepted into the legal systems of the United Kingdom.

Proportionality

In his statement of the grounds for judicial review in English law set out in his speech in the *GCHQ* case, Lord Diplock listed in his own way the generally recognised grounds, but added:[37] 'That is not to say that further developments on a case by case basis may not in course of time add further grounds. I have in mind particularly the possible adoption in the future of the principle of proportionality which is recognised in the administrative law of several of our fellow members of the European Economic Community'. This amounts to an express recognition of the possibility of the deliberate incorporation of principles derived from other Member States of the Community and from Community law itself into English administrative law, but it has to be said that more than a decade later, at the end of 1996, those words could still be quoted verbatim by Aldous LJ.[38]

As noted in Chapter 3, proportionality is a principle which

---

36. [1995] 2 All ER 714.
37. [1984] 3 All ER 935 at p. 950.
38. *R v Radio Authority, ex p Bull* [1997] 2 All ER 561.

would appear to have entered into Community law via German law, where the 'Verhältnismässigkeitsgrundsatz' has been held to be a principle underlying certain provisions of the Basic Law. While its early use in Community law amounted to little more than an assertion with regard to the activities of coal and steel undertakings that the punishment must fit the crime, the classic definition of proportionality in Community administrative law is that given by A.G. Dutheillet de Lamothe in 1970.[39] This is that citizens may only have imposed on them, for the purposes of the public interest, obligations which are strictly necessary for those purposes to be attained.

Although the import of Lord Diplock's remarks is that the principle of proportionality is not one with which English courts are familiar, nevertheless English courts have not been backward in referring questions to the European Court asking whether a particular provision of Community law did breach that principle. This is illustrated by the case of *E.D. and F. Man v Intervention Board*[40] which involved EC legislation requiring a person who successfully tendered for the export of sugar to lodge a security, in this case £1,670,000, to ensure that the export actually took place. Under the terms of the relevant EC Regulation, that security was to be forfeited if an export licence was not applied for within a specified time limit. Man Sugar were for various reasons, three and three-quarter hours late in applying for their export licence, and the English judge, Gladwell J, referred to the European Court the question whether the EC Regulation, in so far as it required the whole security to be forfeited for a failure to apply for the export licence on time, breached the principle of proportionality, particularly since there was still in fact enough time actually to carry out the export transaction. The European Court, as has been seen, held that the principle was indeed breached, a conclusion it reached by applying a purposive interpretation to the relevant regulation. The basis of the decision was that the Court in interpreting the legislation made a distinction between what it regarded as the primary obligation, actually to carry out the export transaction, and the secondary obligation to apply for an export licence within a specific time; in the view of the Court, to penalise a failure to comply with the secondary obligation as severely as a

---

39. Case 11/70 *Internationale Handelsgesellschaft* [1970] ECR 1125 at p. 1148.
40. Case 181/84, [1985] ECR 2889. See Chapter 3 above.

failure to comply with the primary obligation would breach the principle of proportionality.

As has already been indicated, this principle may be applied not only against the Community institutions, but also against national authorities in the context of Community law, and it has thus occurred that the United Kingdom has fallen foul of the principle with regard to measures restricting the movement of goods which were claimed to be justified on grounds of the protection of health under Article 36 of the EC Treaty.

The example was given in Chapter 3 of the rules governing the importation of UHT milk into the United Kingdom.[41] The United Kingdom at the relevant time required that imported UHT milk should be re-treated in the United Kingdom, thereby destroying any economic advantage in importing the stuff and to all intents and purposes constituting a prohibition on imports. The European Court held that the United Kingdom's health requirements could equally well be met by a requirement that importers produce certificates issued by the competent authorities of the exporting Member State, coupled with controls by means of samples.

Another example is the famous poultrymeat case,[42] where a prohibition was imposed in 1981 on imports into Great Britain of poultrymeat and eggs from all other Member States except Denmark and Ireland, allegedly to prevent the outbreak of Newcastle disease. Quite apart from the fact that the European Court took the view that in the circumstances this was not a seriously considered health policy anyway, it stated that the measures taken by the United Kingdom were not proportionate to the objective they pursued. In other words, a total prohibition on imports could only be justified if the United Kingdom could show that that was the only possibility open to it, and the European Court was of the opinion that less stringent measures could have been used.

Apart from matters falling within the scope of Community law, English courts seem also to have been willing to apply a concept of proportionality in relation to the European Convention on Human Rights, to the extent that it might, while not incorporated into the laws of the United Kingdom, be used as an aid to interpretation. In *Derbyshire County Council v Times Newspapers*,[43] Lord Keith of

---

41. Case 124/81 *Commission v UK* [1983] ECR 203.
42. Case 40/82 *Commission v UK* [1982] ECR 2793.
43. [1993] AC 534 at p. 550.

Kinkel cited the jurisprudence of the European Court of Human Rights to hold that for a restriction on freedom of expression under Article 10 of the Convention to be regarded as 'necessary in a democratic society' required the existence of a pressing social need, and the restrictions should be no more than was proportionate to the legitimate aim pursued. The same view was taken with regard to the exceptions to the right to respect for private and family life under Article 8 of the Convention by Hirst LJ in *R v Secretary of State for the Home Department, ex p Hargreaves*.[44]

The question remains, however, of the extent to which acceptance of the principle of proportionality would in reality constitute the acceptance of a novel doctrine into English law. The terminology of proportionality, at least with regard to sanctions, has indeed been used in English law.[45] In *R v Barnsley MBC, ex p Hook*[46] it was held to be disproportionate to ban a market trader, Mr. Hook, from trading at Barnsley market for the rest of his life because he relieved himself in a side street near the market after the public conveniences had closed. More generally, the then President of the European Court, Lord MacKenzie-Stuart, in delivering the presidential address to the Holdsworth Club in the University of Birmingham in 1986,[47] went on record as asking whether proportionality was anything other than the concept of reasonableness. The words 'reasonable' and 'reasonableness' are, of course, part of the stock-in-trade of the legal systems of the United Kingdom, although it might be suggested that they seem to have different meanings in different contexts.

In the context of judicial control of the administration in England, unreasonableness was equated by Lord Diplock in his speech in the *GCHQ* case with irrationality,[48] that is, a decision which is so outrageous in its defiance of logic or of accepted moral standards that no sensible person who had applied his mind to the question to be decided could have arrived at it. If only such conduct is unreasonable, then there is indeed a wide gulf between the English concept of reasonableness and the European Community concept of proportionality. Lord MacKenzie-Stuart suggested that the dif-

---

44. [1997] 1 All ER 397 at p. 413.
45. See Jowell and Lester, 'Proportionality: Neither Novel Nor Dangerous' in Jowell and Oliver (eds), *New Directions in Judicial Review* (London, 1988).
46. [1976] 3 All ER 452.
47. 'Control of Power within the European Communities' (Birmingham, 1986).
48. [1984] 3 All ER 935 at p. 951.

ference was one of degree rather than of substance; might it be submitted that perhaps it is really a difference of emphasis? The concept of reasonableness in English administrative law appears to take as its starting point the rationality or otherwise of the conduct of the authority in question,[49] although of course the consequences of that conduct may be a relevant factor. On the other hand, the European Community concept of proportionality would appear to take as its starting point the consequences of the authorities' actions for the subject of the law, i.e. it asks the question: what is the burden imposed on the subject? – though of course it may take account of the rationality of what the authority did as well.

The consequence is, of course, that a disproportionate burden on the subject of the law may lead to the invalidity of a general policy, and this perhaps explains the continued reluctance to take the principle of proportionality any further in the domestic legal systems of the United Kingdom. As the current Lord Chancellor has put it,[50] the fundamental objection to the incorporation of the principle of proportionality is that, 'it invites review of the merits of public decisions on the basis of a standard which is considerably lower than that of *Wednesbury* reasonableness and would involve the court in a process of policy evaluation which goes far beyond its allotted constitutional role'.

On the other hand, the principle of proportionality has been dismissed as a mere facet of irrationality,[51] and it has been applied at the level of the penalties to be imposed for non-payment of rates (i.e. making the punishment fit the crime).[52] However, the matter was analysed in some detail by Neill LJ in *R v Secretary of State for the Environment, ex p NALGO*.[53] He suggested that there was much to be said for the view that all the courts in the European Community should apply common standards in the field of administrative law, and that in time English courts would become familiar with the principle of proportionality. In his view it could well be that, in cases involving the judicial review of decisions made at

[49]. *Associated Provincial Picture Houses Ltd v Wednesbury Corporation* [1948] 1 KB 223.

[50]. Lord Irvine of Lairg QC, [1996] Public Law 72.

[51]. See e.g. Lord Donaldson MR in *R v Secretary of State for the Home Department, ex p Brind* [1991] 1 AC 697.

[52]. Laws J in *R v Highbury Corner Magistrates' Court, ex p Uchendu* (1994) Times, 28 January.

[53]. (1992) *The Times*, 2 December. The comments discussed are taken from the transcript.

a lower level than government level, the law will develop on the lines that lack of proportionality will come to be recognised as a separate ground of intervention. On the other hand, he saw greater difficulty in applying the principle of proportionality to the decisions of government Ministers, because it would not allow them so many degrees of latitude as that afforded by the traditional *Wednesbury* doctrine.

Conclusion

At the least, the situation has now been reached where judges in the United Kingdom feel able openly to state a willingness to take conscious account of a principle derived from the laws of the other Member States and held to be a general principle of Community law. Even without such conscious recognition, there has been an intriguing degree of parallel development with regard to certain principles in the domestic legal systems of the United Kingdom and in European Community law. Furthermore, use of general principles of Community law has become a back-door method by which the principles of the European Convention on Human Rights may be enforced in the United Kingdom pending its formal incorporation. But perhaps most notable of all, in the context of techniques of interpretation there appears to have been a quiet revolution, so that what was once described as a strange system from which no assistance could be derived appears to be used virtually on a daily basis even in the context of lawyers' law.

Familiar as Lord Denning's metaphors about incoming tides may be in the context of European Community law,[54] a passage of nineteenth-century poetry by A. H. Clough[55] is perhaps more apposite in the present context:

> For while the tired waves, vainly breaking,
> seem here no painful inch to gain,
> Far back through creeks and inlets making,
> comes silent, flooding in, the main.

---

54. See *Bulmer v Bollinger* [1974] 2 All ER 1226.
55. *Say not the Struggle Naught Availeth*.

Further reading

Arnull: *The general principles of EEC law and the individual* (Pinter 1989)

Coppell and O'Neill: *The European Court of Justice: Taking Rights Seriously?* (1992) CML Rev. 669

Dauses: *The protection of fundamental rights in the Community legal order* (1985) EL Rev. 398

De Burca: *The Principle of Proportionality and its Application in Community Law* (1993) 13 YEL 105

De Burca: 'The Language of Rights and European Integration' in Shaw and More (eds) *New Legal Dynamics of European Union* (Clarendon, Oxford, 1995)

Edward: 'The Role and Relevance of the Civil Law Tradition in the Work of the European Court of Justice' in Carey Miller and Zimmermann (eds) *The Civilian Tradition and Scots Law* (Duncker and Humblot, Berlin, 1997)

Ellis: *The Definition of Discrimination in European Community Sex Equality Law* (1994) EL Rev. 563

Emiliou: *The principle of proportionality in European Law* (Kluwer, London, 1996)

Herdegen: *The Relation between the Principles of Equality and Proportionality* (1985) 22 CML Rev. 683

Schwarze: *European Administrative Law* (Sweet and Maxwell, London, 1992)

Sharpston: *Legitimate Expectations and Economic Reality* (1990) 15 EL Rev. 103

Usher: *The influence of national concepts on decisions of the European Court of Justice* (1976) EL Rev 359

Usher: *Principles derived from private law and the European Court of Justice* (1993) European Review of Private Law 109

Usher: The influence of the Civil Law, via Modern Legal Systems, on European Community Law' in Carey Miller and Zimmermann (eds) *The Civilian Tradition and Scots Law* (Duncker and Humblot, Berlin, 1997)

Watson: *Equality of Treatment: A Variable Concept?* (1995) 24 ILJ 33

Weiler and Lockhart: *Taking rights seriously – the ECJ and its fundamental rights jurisprudence* (1995) 32 CMLR 51 and 579

Bibliography

Bebr, 'Direct and indirect control of Community acts in practice' in *The Art of Governance, Festschrift in honour of Eric Stein* (1987)

Cardwell, *Milk Quotas* (Oxford, 1996)

Craig, 'Substantive Legitimate Expectations in Domestic and Community Law' (1996) CLJ 289

Dembour, *Droit Administratif (Liège)*

Emiliou, *The Principle of Proportionality in European Law* (Kluwer, London, 1996)

Fennell, 'Community Preference and Developing Countries' (1997) European Foreign Affairs Review 235

Forsthoff, *Lehrbuch des Verwaltungsrechts* (Munich)

Green, Hartley and Usher, *The Legal Foundations of the Single European Market* (Oxford, 1991)

Hamson, *Methods of interpretation – a critical assessment of the results*, Reports of the Judicial and Academic Conference (Luxembourg, 1976)

Jowell and Lester, 'Proportionality: Neither Novel Nor Dangerous' in Jowell and Oliver (eds), *New Directions in Judicial Review* (London, 1988)

Kelly, *Fundamental Rights in the Irish Law and Constitution* (Dublin, 1961)

Schiemann, Lord Justice, 'The Application of General Principles of Community Law by English Courts', The European Advocate, Winter Issue 1996/7

Schmidt-Bleibtrau and Klein *Kommentar zum Grundgesetz* (Luchterhand, Neuwied, 6th edition 1983)

Schwarze, *European Administrative Law* (London, 1992)

Temple Lang, *The Duties of National Courts under the Constitutional Law of the European Community* (Exeter, 1987)

Toth, Steiner and Emiliou papers in O'Keeffe and Twomey (eds), *Legal Issues of the Maastricht Treaty* (Chichester, 1994)

Usher, 'Establishment, Services and Lawyers' (1979) *Scots Law Times* 65

Usher, 'The Influence of National Concepts on Decisions of the European Court' (1976) EL Rev. 359

Usher, 'Judicial Review of Community Acts and the Private Litigant' in Campbell and Voyatzi (eds) *Legal Reasoning and Judicial Interpretation of European Law – Essays in honour of Lord Mackenzie-Stuart* (Trenton, 1996)

Usher, *Legal Aspects of Agriculture in the European Community* (Oxford, 1988)

Vedel, *Droit Administratif* (Paris, 1973)

Waline, *Droit Administratif* (Paris, 9th edition, 1969)

Waline, *Livre Jubilaire* (Luxembourg, 1957)

Index